COOKING
KOSHER

COOKING
KOSHER

THE ILLUSTRATED GUIDE TO JEWISH FOOD, WITH OVER 75 TRADITIONAL RECIPES

MARLENA SPIELER

HERMES HOUSE

This edition is published by Hermes House, an imprint of Anness Publishing Ltd, Hermes House, 88–89 Blackfriars Road, London SE1 8HA; tel. 020 7401 2077; fax 020 7633 9499

www.hermeshouse.com; www.annesspublishing.com

If you like the images in this book and would like to investigate using them for publishing, promotions or advertising, please visit our website www.practicalpictures.com for more information.

Publisher: Joanna Lorenz
Managing Editor: Linda Fraser
Junior Editor: Laura Seber
Photographer: William Lingwood
Designer: Nigel Partridge
Production Controller: Darren Price

ETHICAL TRADING POLICY

At Anness Publishing we believe that business should be conducted in an ethical and ecologically sustainable way, with respect for the environment and a proper regard to the replacement of the natural resources we employ.
As a publisher, we use a lot of wood pulp in high-quality paper for printing, and that wood commonly comes from spruce trees.
We are therefore currently growing more than 750,000 trees in three Scottish forest plantations: Berrymoss (130 hectares/320 acres), West Touxhill (125 hectares/305 acres) and Deveron Forest (75 hectares/185 acres). The forests we manage contain more than 3.5 times the number of trees employed each year in making paper for the books we manufacture.
Because of this ongoing ecological investment programme, you, as our customer, can have the pleasure and reassurance of knowing that a tree is being cultivated on your behalf to naturally replace the materials used to make the book you are holding.
Our forestry programme is run in accordance with the UK Woodland Assurance Scheme (UKWAS) and will be certified by the internationally recognized Forest Stewardship Council (FSC). The FSC is a non-government organization dedicated to promoting responsible management of the world's forests. Certification ensures forests are managed in an environmentally sustainable and socially responsible way. For further information about this scheme, go to www.annesspublishing.com/trees

PUBLISHER'S NOTE

Although the advice and information in this book are believed to be accurate and true at the time of going to press, neither the authors nor the publisher can accept any legal responsibility or liability for any errors or omissions that may have been made nor for any inaccuracies nor for any loss, harm or injury that comes about from following instructions or advice in this book.

NOTES

Bracketed terms are intended for American readers.
For all recipes, quantities are given in both metric and imperial measures and, where appropriate, in standard cups and spoons.
Follow one set of measures, but not a mixture, because they are not interchangeable.
Standard spoon and cup measures are level. 1 tsp = 5ml, 1 tbsp = 15ml, 1 cup = 250ml/8fl oz.
Australian standard tablespoons are 20ml. Australian readers should use 3 tsp in place of 1 tbsp for measuring small quantities.
American pints are 16fl oz/2 cups. American readers should use 20fl oz/2.5 cups in place of 1 pint when measuring liquids.
Electric oven temperatures in this book are for conventional ovens. When using a fan oven, the temperature will probably need to be reduced by about 10–20°C/20–40°F. Since ovens vary, you should check with your manufacturer's instruction book for guidance.
Medium (US large) eggs are used unless otherwise stated.

Main front cover image shows stuffed vine leaves with cumin, lemon and herbs – for recipe, see page 82.

Previously published as *Kosher Cooking*

CONTENTS

There is no festive celebration without eating and drinking

THE TALMUD

Jewish food. The phrase conjures up images of borscht, chicken soup with matzo balls, salt beef and chopped liver. These certainly are Jewish foods, relished by generations of Eastern European Jews, but the Jewish cuisine is much, much more varied than that.

I grew up in California. The foods we ate were those of West Coast America – artichokes and oranges and avocados – but our culinary souls were also nourished by the foods of the Old Country of our grandparents' era: *kasha*, *gedempte flaiche* and *knaidlach*, *matzo brei* and *kishke* from Ashkenazi Russia, Poland, Ukraine and Lithuania, all served with a delicious overlay of Old New York.

Jewish food is a combination of richly varied cuisines from all over the globe, reflecting the multi-ethnicity of the Jewish people, and the many places where they have settled. For years I thought the little savoury pastries called *empanadas* were typically Jewish, because that's what my cousin used to make when we visited her. It was only years later that I discovered they were native to Uruguay, where she was raised. One of my friends, whose family fled Germany to South America because of World War II, and who grew up eating her grandmother's food, told me she thought that Jewish food was *mole*, that typically Mexican dish. And so it is, at least for Mexican Jews.

In the past, the Ashkenazim and Sephardim were often far removed from each other; the spicy food of the Sephardim was seldom served on traditional Ashkenazi tables and vice versa. The establishment of the State of Israel, migration and modern travel have changed this considerably, and brought Jews together again, starting at the table where they can share their own flavours and dishes.

Regardless of where history has taken them, the food Jews eat is governed by the laws of Kashrut – the code of fitness that applies to what may be eaten, how food must be prepared and which foods can be combined with other foods. There are variations in how different ethnic groups adhere to Kashrut, and degrees of observance, but the basics are the same. Certain types of meat, fish and fowl are allowed, while others are forbidden. Rules govern the slaughter and inspection of animals, as well as which parts may be used, and there is an injunction against combining meat foods with dairy foods. This set of rules has kept the Jewish people culturally distinct, as well as giving an underlying flavour to their food.

The preparation, eating and rituals involved with Kashrut have always played an important part in the lives of the Jewish people. In the Torah, the Patriarch Abraham is noted for the hospitable table he sets. It is recorded that Isaac asked his son for a nice dish of savoury meat, and also that Esau sold his birthright for a big, soupy lentil stew. In Chapter 11 of the book of Numbers, the story is told of how the Israelites fleeing Egypt wept with longing for the garlic and leeks they had eaten during their captivity – even freedom lacked flavour without delicious seasonings.

The noted Andalucian-Egyptian philosopher and physician Moses Maimonides (Moses ben Maimon) emphasized the importance of serenity of spirit, both for cook and diner. He also stressed the value of eating healthy food, prepared appealingly. Sharing sociable meals, he suggested, not only made for a happier, less anxious individual; it also bridged the differences between ethnic groups.

When Jews gather together, we eat, and what we eat are often the traditional foods, because each food has its own story. The flavour of remembrance seasons all our meals as we recall where we have wandered and who we met along the way, the meals we shared and the ingredients that filled our pots along each mile, in every place.

Even in terrible times of deprivation and despair, we like to prepare special foods. I was very touched when a Holocaust survivor told me how she and her companions had once made pancakes using greens that grew wild on a tiny patch of earth. Under cover of darkness, they had picked the greens, patted them into little cakes and fried them in a drop or two of oil. "Ach", her eyes lit up, "they were so good."

For Jews, eating is a celebration of survival. A meal enjoyed with family, friends and community means "we are alive", and we are grateful. A basic tenet of the Jewish table is that good food is a gift from God. Jews take every opportunity of offering thanks and appreciation, with blessings for the food and also for the good health that allows them to enjoy it. However different, culturally, Jews might be, we are united by beliefs and laws, as well as an interwoven history – in the way we pray, speak, eat, drink and celebrate life; the laws of Kashrut that guide what we eat and how we prepare it; and the prayers that sanctify it all. Our food is more than just a cuisine represented by recipes; it is a part of the glue that holds us together.

In this book I would like to share with you my favourite recipes from various Jewish communities throughout the world, and from my own life and traditions as well. In the words of the Hebrew expression that translates as *bon appetit*, I wish you all *B'tay avon*. MARLENA SPIELER

THE JEWISH DIASPORA

Exile has been a common thread throughout the history of the Jewish people. It is this, linked with intrinsic religious and cultural considerations, that has been a major factor in developing a cuisine that is as diverse as it is delicious. As communities fled from one country to another, they took with them their culinary traditions but also adopted new ones along the way.

With the destruction by the Romans of the Second Temple in Jerusalem in 70CE (AD), the Jews were banished from their holy city. Since that date, they have travelled the world, establishing communities, many of which lasted for centuries, before being forced to flee once more.

Jews spread to nearly every corner of the globe and this dispersal or diaspora has helped to create the cultural and liturgical differences that exist within a single people. Following the dispersal, two important Jewish communities were established, which still define the two main Jewish groups that exist today: the Sephardim and the Ashkenazim who each have their own individual culture, cuisine and liturgy.

The first of these communites was in Iberia, called Sepharad after a city in Asia Minor mentioned in Obadiah 20. The second was in the Rhine River Valley and was called Ashkenaz, after a kingdom on the upper Euphrates, which is referred to in Jeremiah 51:27.

Iberia, which was ruled by Muslims, was a relatively tolerant society. The Jews had a revered place in it, living undisturbed and in harmony with their Islamic neighbours for long periods of time. Jews also often held influential positions as doctors, scholars or advisers to the kings.

In contrast, the Christian lands of Europe were restrictive, feudal, and often hostile. The Ashkenazim tended to live apart in ghettos or shtetl (villages) away from the non-Jewish population with whom they had settled. They also spoke a different language from their neighbours and became very strict regarding their dietary laws as they were surrounded by people who ate pork, rabbit, shellfish and other non-kosher foods that were forbidden to Jews.

Over the centuries both communities blossomed in their new environments, but each developed very differently, creating their own cultures. Ashkenazi Jews developed different customs, laws,

Below: A painting by Francesco Hayez depicting the destruction of the Jewish Temple in Jerusalem by the Romans under Titus in 70CE (AD) (1867).

liturgy, Hebrew pronunciations and cooking styles from their Sephardi cousins, despite having the same roots in the Babylonian Talmud.

Yemenite Jews, known as Taymanim, are the third largest Jewish ethnic group today. Although, historically, they do not belong to the Sephardim, they are often grouped with them, possibly because of their Eastern culture and traditional spicy cuisine. Other ethnic groups that are not either Ashkenazi nor Sephardi include Jewish communities from Iran, Azerbaijan, Bukhara (Uzbekistan), Georgia (Russia), Kurdistan, India, Ethiopia and K'ai-feng (Canton).

THE SEPHARDIM

Jews who settled in Iberia spoke Ladino, a dialect of Castilian Spanish written in Hebrew script. In many respects, their lifestyle was not so very different from that of their Arab neighbours, who had a similar outlook of generous hospitality. The Arabs also prepared their food ritually: meat was ridded of blood and pork was forbidden.

Jews lived in Jewish Quarters, which were known as mellahs, generally by choice. This helped to strengthen their culture and community and allowed them to be near the centres of Jewish life such as the synagogue, kosher butcher and ritual baths.

As the Iberian Jews settled and moved, four main groups emerged. Judeo-Spanish Jews settled in the Ottoman lands of Turkey and Greece. Maghrebi or North African Jews settled in Morocco, Tunisia, Algeria and Libya. Arab Jews lived in Babylon and Persia and, for over ten centuries, Iraqi and Babylonian Jews were the leaders of world Jewry. Syria, Iraq, Lebanon and Iran all produced Jewish communities of greatness – centres of excellence for culture, learning and commerce.

The communities could have grown in different directions but the caravan trade allowed communication and mobility between the different groups. Matters of Rabbinical law, politics and business exchanged hands easily. Migration in search of new opportunities also became common.

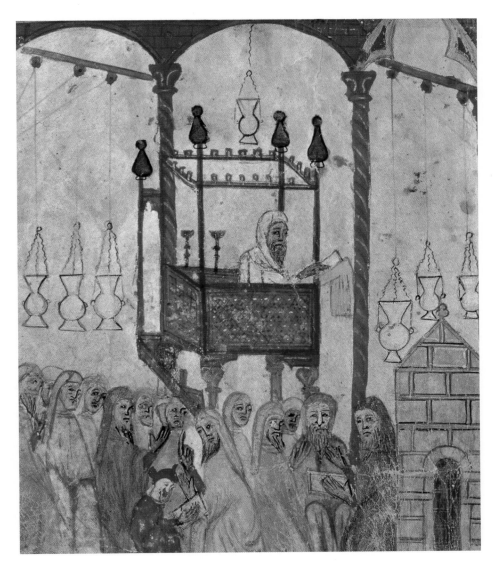

This interaction between the different communities allowed a mingling and unification of flavours in the Sephardi cuisine. The food the Sephardi Jews ate, and the way they cooked it, was a blend of their own heritage and dietary laws, with distinct influences from the Iberian and Arabic culinary tradition. What emerged was a cuisine rich with the flavours of the region.

At its heart, Sephardi cooking still has the warm undertones of Spain: it is olive oil-based, rich with fish from the sea and the vegetables of a warm climate, fragrant with garlic, herbs and spices. When meat is used, it is usually lamb.

The Sephardim also introduced their own influences on the Iberian and Arab cuisines. Even today, if you enquire in

Above: An illumination from a Hebrew manuscript showing a synagogue in northern Spain (c.1350).

Andalucia in Spain as to what have been the major influences on their cuisine, the Jewish contribution will always be acknowledged alongside that of the Moors.

Sephardi cooking reflected Sephardi life: sensual and embued with life's pleasures. This attitude went further than just the food. It is reflected in the celebrations for life's happy occasions too. For instance, in Sephardi tradition, a wedding celebration lasted for two weeks, and a Brit Milah or Bar Mitzvah celebration lasted for a week. These traditions live still on today.

Morocco, Egypt and Romania, they acquired a love of new and often exotic flavourings, and when they moved on, whether by choice or because they were forced to do so, they took their recipes with them. For instance, when Iraqi Sephardi Jews migrated to India in the 19th century, they introduced Middle Eastern flavours to the Bene Israel and Cochinese Jews already there. They used spices in ways unknown before, and these methods were embraced enthusiastically by the Indian Jews.

Left: North African Sephardi Jews wear traditional prayer shawls in a synagogue on the island of Djerba off the coast of Tunisia (1952).

Below: A Jewish grocer in a Moroccan souk (market) sells the specialities of his community.

Into Exile Again

The Sephardim, who had flourished in Spain for centuries, now found the tide beginning to turn against them. Shortly before the end of the 14th century, antagonism erupted into violent riots and thousands of Jews were massacred.

Many of those who survived were forced, on pain of death, to convert. These Jews were known as conversos or – less politely – marranos, which means pork eater. They and their families often continued their religious practices in secret. At times such as these, food was a great comfort, not only because eating familiar, traditional dishes reminded conversos of their history, but also because, in their own kitchens, they could observe the rituals bound up with preparation and serving.

For a few decades these clandestine Jews flourished but they were a thorn in the flesh of the Spanish rulers and led to the Spanish Inquisition at the end of the 15th century. In 1492 all the remaining Jews in Spain were expelled. They scattered to North Africa, Europe, the Middle East and the New World.

With each migration, Sephardi Jews encountered new flavours, which they introduced into their own cooking. From countries such as Iraq, Turkey, Greece,

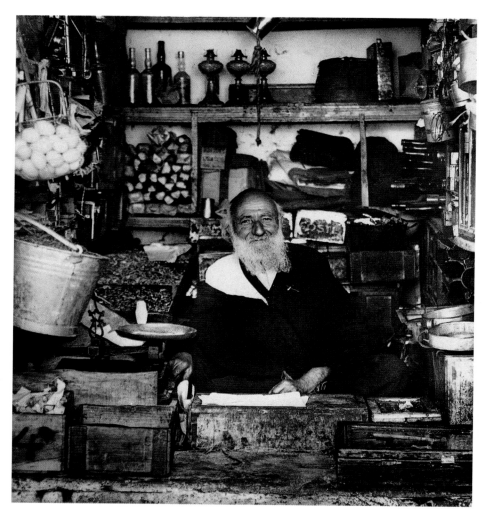

THE ASHKENAZIM

The Jews who fled to the Rhine Valley were, over the centuries, to spread across Europe. Ashkenazi Jewish communities of France, Italy and Germany, which were so numerous in the early Middle Ages, were pushed further and further eastwards due to persecutions from the time of the Crusades, which began early in the 11th century. Many Jews fled to Eastern Europe, especially Poland. They spoke Yiddish, which is a combination of Middle High German and Hebrew, written in Hebrew script.

Their non-Jewish neighbours ate abundant shellfish and pork, cooked with lard, and mixed milk with meat freely, none of which was permitted for Jews, so the only answer for them was to keep themselves apart. In Czarist Russia, they were only allowed to live in the Pale of Settlement, a portion of land that stretched from the Baltic Sea to the Black Sea. The Ashkenazi Jews lived – often uneasily – in shtetl (villages) and never knew when they would be forced to flee again.

For the Jews who settled in Germany and Austria, the age of enlightenment was the Haskalah (18th–19th century), when the reform movement freed them from the more restrictive bonds of religious adherence and allowed them to enter the secular world of arts, philosophy, science and music. German Jews amassed great knowledge and created a culture of depth and finesse. They became so intertwined with the culture of Germany that when the Holocaust was upon them they could not fathom how it could have happened, because they considered themselves German first and foremost.

Ashkenazi food was the food of a cold climate. Vegetables were pickled in salt and fermented, for instance cabbage became sauerkraut, which was stored to last the winter. Cucumbers were transformed into pickles, piquant treats to enliven the bland fare of winter. Fermented beetroot (beets) became

Right: A group of Ashkenazi Jews sit outside their home in Jerusalem (1885).

russel, the basis for a traditional borscht. Fish – freshwater, rather than the sea fish enjoyed by the Sephardi Jews – were smoked and salted, as were meats. Because there was often insufficient kosher meat to go round, very small amounts would be bulked out with other ingredients and served as dumplings and pastries, or in casseroles and stews.

Grains and beans were eaten in abundance: healthy, hearty and filling, they were also pareve, so they could be mixed with either meat or milk. Often, but most usually for Shabbat or a festival, beans were cooked slowly with meats in a dish known as cholent, which could be eaten when the family returned home from the synagogue.

Horseradish was shredded into an eye-watering condiment, and fresh herbs and other aromatics such as spring onions (scallions), dill and parsley were delighted in.

Ashkenazi food was often cooked in chicken or goose fat, enriched with golden onions. It was sometimes flavoured with honey, or a mixture of honey and piquant vinegar, to make a tangy sweet and sour sauce.

When potatoes were introduced from the New World, the Ashkenazi Jews adored them and incorporated them into their cuisine with great enthusiasm. Latkes and kugels, soups and dumplings were all prepared from this new and filling vegetable.

JEWS IN BRITAIN

The history of the Jews in Britain is long and complex. They first arrived in 1066 and were expelled by Edward I in 1290, a hundred years after the massacre at Clifford Tower of York's entire Jewish community. In 1655, after negotiations had been held between Manashe ben Israel and Oliver Cromwell, Jews were allowed to return and live in England.

Sephardi Jews then came to settle in England. They came via Holland, bringing with them the flavours and specialities of their native Portugal, which included their favourite dish, battered or crumbed fried fish. This was very likely the origin of Britain's traditional fish and chips, as the fish was subsequently combined with fried potatoes and eaten by the hungry masses – mostly Jews, often young women who worked in sweat shops in London's East End.

Today, most of Britain's Jewish communities live in London, specifically north London, with smaller communities scattered around the rest of the country, including Brighton, Essex, Manchester, Liverpool, Glasgow and Edinburgh. Stamford Hill in north London is home to one of the largest communities of Chassidic Jews in the world. Most of the Jewish communities in Britain are Ashkenazi, though there are a few Sephardi groups.

INFLUENCING THE FRENCH CUISINE

The French cuisine shows a strong influence from the Jewish community that settled there. Foie gras, often considered to be typically French, originated in ancient Egypt and was undoubtedly introduced to France by Jewish immigrants – Ashkenazim in Alsace, and possibly by Sephardim in the south-west.

Some say the cassoulet of south-west France was originally cholent, the bean and meat stew baked slowly in a low oven and served still warm on Shabbat; and that the spices that are so well loved in eastern France – cumin, ginger and cinnamon – are testament to the Jewish community that flourished there. Chocolate, like aubergines (eggplant), came to France with the Sephardi Jews expelled from Spain.

Chassidic Jews

This group of very observant Jews, recognizable by their traditional Eastern European dress – black coats for the men, large hats of either black cloth or fur, and often scarves covering the women's hair – originated in Central Poland, Galicia and Ukraine. The movement was founded by Israel ben Eliezer, also known as the Ba'al Shem Tov (master of the good name), in the 17th century.

A JEWISH HERITAGE IN ITALY

The Italian Jewish community (Italkim), which is now very small as a result of the Holocaust and post-World War II emigration, was once grand, influential and active. It is said that the true Roman is the Jewish Roman, for there has been a Jewish community in Rome for longer than any other. The Italian cuisine has been influenced very strongly by these long-established settlers. To this day, carciofi alla Giudia (artichokes in the Jewish manner) is a speciality of the ghetto of Rome, *ghetto* being a word that originated in Italy to describe an area set aside for Jews.

The little town of Pitigliano in Tuscany was once such an important centre of Jewish life, religious study and culture that it was known as Little Jerusalem. The Jewish community built the aqueduct, and the matzo ovens they used are still there. During World War II, the Jews of Pitigliano were saved by local people, who smuggled them out of the city and hid them in the countryside. Although there are no Jews there now, all of them having emigrated to either America or Israel, the citizens of Pitigliano rejoice in the fact that Jews from Israel often come to their town to be married in the synagogue there.

Left: Jews struggling to make a living in London's East End (1900s).

Opposite: A bakery selling matzos in the Jewish area in the 4th arrondissement of Paris (1923).

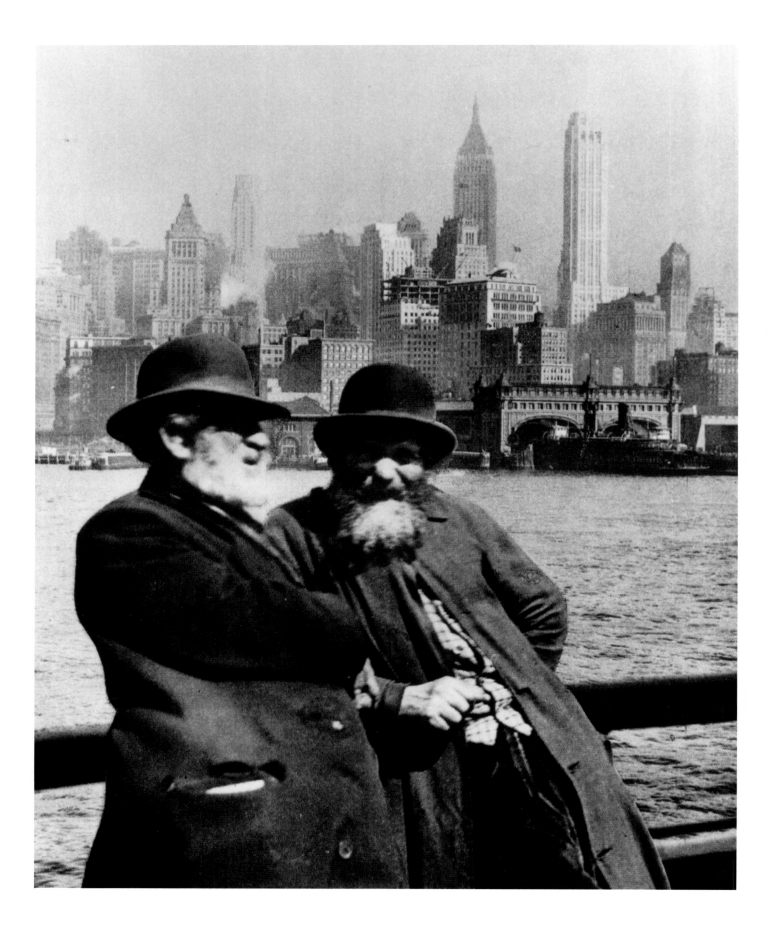

THE UNITED STATES AND THE DELI

In the early part of the 20th century there was a great wave of immigration to the United States, which influenced the American table a great deal. The most obvious influence was the emergence of the delicatessen – or deli as it is more commonly known. In places that were home to Jewish communities from Eastern Europe, such as Chicago and Old New York, delis were places where hungry men with no homes of their own could go for a good meal. These men had usually travelled ahead – often years ahead – of their wives and children to establish a new life. Lodging in rented rooms and working hard to save enough money to pay for their families to join them, they needed somewhere to eat that was kosher, and that gave them a taste of the land they left behind.

Other ethnic groups discovered delis and began to enjoy the hearty foods they served, which became the flavour of America: bagels, soups, pastrami and other robust meats, huge sandwiches, dill pickles, salads and juicy sausages.

MODERN TIMES

The 20th century saw the end of many of the great Jewish communities of the world – some as old as 2,500 years – and the start of others. Ashkenazim emigrating from Germany, Central Europe and Russia towards the end of the 19th century and the start of the 20th century often packed little by way of possessions, but they did take the traditions of the cuisine that we typically think of as Jewish: chicken soup and matzo balls, Viennese pastries, rye bread and bagels, delicate noodles and robust chopped liver. The same dishes – familiarly called the food of the Old Country – travelled to Great Britain, Israel, Latin America and the United States with the refugees before, during and after World War II.

Left: Jewish immigrants stand on Ellis Island, awaiting entry into New York.

Right: The Jewish deli is a wonderful legacy from the Ashkenazi Jews who settled in the United States.

The Holocaust destroyed much of European Jewish culture, and the Communist control of Eastern Europe and Russia swept away most of the remainder, although here and there communities continued to keep the faith, albeit in secret, allowing their traditions to survive.

In many places, communities have regrouped. In Los Angeles you will find the Jewish community of Iran, reborn after the Islamic revolution. This community had been in Persia since 600BCE (BC) and held tight to their customs and cuisine. In Brooklyn, a suburb of New York, there is a thriving Cochinese synagogue, where Indian Jews cook their spicy delicacies for feast celebrations. In Cochin itself there are barely a handful of Jews left. In the Israeli port of Jaffa, you can eat wonderfully spicy, zesty Libyan food

thanks to Libyan Jews who have relocated and settled there. In Beijing in China, a fledgling synagogue and Jewish community have recently emerged, consisting primarily of international workers and their families.

Traditionally, when Sephardi and Ashkenazi Jews settled in the same country, they tended to keep apart, maintaining their distinctive cultures, but that too has changed in recent times. When Askenazim from Eastern Europe and Germany emigrated to South America, they frequently found themselves living alongside Sephardi Jews from Spain. Conversely, Sephardim from North Africa moved to France after World War II and helped to breathe new life into the Ashkenazi communities destroyed by Hitler.

A NEW HOME IN ISRAEL

With the establishment of the State of Israel in 1948, hundreds of thousands of Jews who had been both isolated and stateless for generations made their way back. Each group brought with them the ways of cooking and the flavours of the countries in which they had been living.

At first, this diversity wasn't always appreciated. The halutzim (settlers) were eager to be integrated and to divorce themselves from a past that included what they saw as the foods of bondage. There was great pressure to abandon individual traditions and other cultures, to throw all into one melting pot labelled Israeli food.

Luckily, at last, all this is changing. Moroccan Jews in Israel are beginning to celebrate their traditional flavours, recognizing that they are delicious in their difference, and not something to be ashamed of. Yemeni restaurants are terribly chic, as are other ethnic eating

houses. The waves of recent Russian and Ethiopian immigrations (the last of Ethiopia's ancient tribe of Jews were flown to Israel in 1992) have added their own ingredients to a cuisine that includes flavours from almost every corner of the globe, set against a background of the Middle East and a belief that what grows easily tastes best.

In an almost complete circle, Ashkenazi food has found a certain cachet in Israel in recent years, with classic dishes such as cholent, chicken soup with matzo balls and pickled vegetables reaching almost cult status. However, in the marvellous fusion of foods that has arisen with the bringing together of the various different Jewish communities, Israeli Ashkenazim have been influenced by other cuisines. For example, classic chicken soup might come with a spoonful of hot and spicy zchug, the Yemenite sauce made of garlic and fiery chillies.

Above: Yemenite Jews look at their new homeland, Lydda in Israel (1950).

Below: Jewish refugees crowd on the top deck of the Haviva Reik *as they arrive in Palestine (1946).*

JEWS TODAY

It is at times of both celebration and commemoration that Jewish cooking really comes into its own, whether the occasion be the weekly Sabbath meal, an annual festival such as Chanukkah or Pesach or one of the events that mark the cycle of Jewish life – such as Brit Milah (ritual circumcision), Bar or Bat Mitzvah (the coming of age), a wedding or a funeral.

Many Jewish families celebrate the traditional religious holidays, but do not necessarily keep kosher or are Shomer Shabbat (those who strictly observe the Sabbath). Thus all over the world, but especially in the USA, where Reform (Progressive) Judaism has become

mainstream, there are many different ways of being Jewish other than being strictly Observant.

In the modern world, many Jews are beginning to adapt their traditions, and they are also making changes in terms of their cuisine. For example, Ashkenazi Jews often use olive oil for cooking, as in the ancient Sephardi tradition. The dishes of the Middle East are also enjoying a resurgence of popularity, and convenience foods are used when time is short.

The laws of Kashrut continue to be a focus of daily life for Observant Jews. In recent years, in addition to traditional Jewish homes, there has been a strong emergence of modern Orthodox Jews,

Above: Yemenite Jews in Jerusalem enjoy a traditional Pesach Seder meal. (Photograph by David Harris.)

those who are returning to a strict adherence to Kashrut, especially in the USA and Israel.

Whether the traditional Jewish table is Sephardi, Ashkenazi, Conservative, Reform (Progressive), Orthodox or Chassidic is not what matters most. The most important factor is that the food it holds reflects both a people's lives and its culture. It is food for enjoying and for bringing families closer together, for giving reassurance in an ever-changing world and for sharing with old and new friends alike.

THE LAWS OF KASHRUT

Kashrut is the set of ritual dietary laws set out in the Bible and the Talmud. Food that conforms to those standards is described as kosher. Whether a Jew comes from a land where onions, garlic and chicken fat are freely eaten, or one whose cuisine includes hot peppers, spices and olive oil, the meals eaten in the Observant Jewish household will not taste the same as food prepared from similar ingredients by non-Jewish neighbours, because the former will conform to the rules of Kashrut.

Though the basic principles of Kashrut are outlined in the Bible, they have been ruled upon by rabbis and codified in the Shulhan Aruckh, the code of Jewish law. No reason is given for the laws of Kashrut, though some rabbinical authorities suggest that hygiene, food safety and health might be contributory factors. Others state, however, that no reason or rationale is needed; obeying the laws of Kashrut is a commandment from God.

Below (clockwise from top): Beef, goat and lamb, when prepared appropriately, are all permitted by the laws of Kashrut.

PERMITTED MEATS

Only certain types of meat are allowed, based on the text in Leviticus 11:3, which states: "Whatsoever parteth the hoof, and is clovenfooted, and cheweth the cud…that shall ye eat." These two conditions mean that ox, sheep, goat, hart, gazelle, roebuck, antelope and mountain sheep may be eaten, while pork, horse and camel are forbidden. No birds or animals of prey are allowed, nor are scavengers, vermin (such as rabbits) creeping insects or reptiles.

PERMITTED BIRDS

The Torah is not quite so clear when it comes to identifying which birds may be eaten. Instead, it lists 24 species of forbidden fowl, which are mainly birds of prey or scavengers. Permitted fowl have in common with each other a protruding claw, a crop and a stomach that can be peeled readily of its inner lining. In general, chicken, duck, turkey and goose are allowed, but this can vary: goose has been popular among Ashkenazim, while Yemenite Jews consider it to be of both the land and sea and therefore forbidden by Kashrut.

Above: Goose is very popular among Eastern European Jews who, in the past, often raised them for their fat livers and to serve at holiday meals.

RITUAL SLAUGHTER

For kosher animals to become kosher meat, they must be slaughtered by the ritual known as *shechita*. An animal that dies of natural causes, or is killed by another animal, is forbidden. The knife for slaughter must be twice as long as the animal's throat and extremely sharp and smooth; even the tiniest nick in the blade renders the knife invalid for kosher butchering. The *shochet* (ritual slaughterer) must sever the animal's trachea and oesophagus without grazing the spine, and the knife must be wielded with care and speed; the smallest delay would bring terror and pain to the animal, rendering the meat unkosher.

The shochet inspects the incision to make sure the cut is smooth, and the lungs must be examined for symptoms of disease. If there is any doubt, the shochet blows air into the lungs; if they fail to hold the air, the animal is not kosher. Certain types of injury also render the animal unkosher. Some cuts of meat are considered unkosher unless specially treated: for example, hind-quarter meat must have the veins and sinews removed in a process known as porging.

Kashering Meat

This is the term used to describe the removal of blood from an animal immediately after slaughter, which is essential if the meat is to be labelled kosher. To Jews, blood is a symbol of life, and the prohibition against consuming it comes from the scriptures: "Therefore I said unto the children of Israel, No soul of you shall eat blood…" (Leviticus 17:12).

Because blood is categorically forbidden by the laws of Kashrut, all meat must be kashered by soaking, salting or grilling (broiling) so that no blood remains. Hearts must be cut open, all veins removed and drained of blood. This is usually done by the butcher. It is then salted and prepared as desired. A spot of blood in an egg renders it unkosher.

How to Kasher Meat

Most kosher butchers kasher meat before offering it for sale. If your butcher does not do this, consult a rabbinical authority or follow the simple instructions below.

1 Place the meat or poultry in a large bowl or bucket as soon as possible after purchase, pour over cold water to cover and leave to stand for 30 minutes.

2 Remove the meat or poultry from the water and place on a plastic drainer, tilted to allow the juices to drain away. Leave to stand for about 5 minutes, then sprinkle with coarse kosher salt. Leave to stand for 1 hour.

3 Rinse the meat three times to rid it of all blood and salt. Pat dry with kitchen paper, then chill until ready to cook.

To kasher liver, rinse it well under cold water, then sprinkle with salt and grill (broil) on a rack or over an open fire, on each side until the flesh is cooked through.

PERMITTED FISH

To be considered kosher, all fish must have detachable scales and fins. Fish with scales that do not come away from the skin are not kosher: "These shall ye eat of all that are in the waters: whatsoever hath fins and scales in the waters, in the seas, and in the rivers, them shall ye eat" (Leviticus 11:9).

The London Bet Din lists the following as being non-kosher fish: abbot, allmouth, angelfish, angler, beluga, blonde, catfish, caviar, cockles, conger eel, crabs, dogfish, eelpout, eels, fiddlefish, fishing frog, frog-fish, glake, goosefish, guffer eel, huss, lumpfish, monkfish, mussels, ray, rigg, rock salmon, rockfish, roker, sea devil, sea pout, skate, sturgeon, swordfish, thornback ray and turbot. Other sea creatures that are forbidden by the laws of Kashrut include all shellfish and crustaceans, sea urchin, octopus and squid.

Below (from left): Red mullet, trout and salmon all have detachable scales so are considered kosher.

Kashrut Certification

To be sure that any packaged food is kosher, look for a symbol of recognized certification every time you buy, as additives and methods can change. There are numerous certifying boards, and many Jews will eat only packaged foods certified by specific boards. If a food is certified as Glatt Kosher it conforms to a particularly stringent kashrut, which requires, among other things, that the lungs be more thoroughly examined.

Some Observant Jews will eat foods such as canned tomatoes, for the only ingredients are tomatoes and salt. Others avoid such foods, as they could have been contaminated on the production line.

Strictly Orthodox Jews will consume sugar and milk products only if they display the rabbinical supervision marking that shows they are untainted by unkosher food or insects.

DAIRY PRODUCTS

Deuteronomy states "Thou shalt not seethe a kid in his mother's milk." This is the basis for the rule that dairy foods and meat must not be cooked together. After eating a meat meal, a certain amount of time must elapse before dairy food can be consumed. Some communities wait six hours, while others wait only two. One only has to wait 30 minutes after eating a dairy meal before having a meat one.

There are many non-dairy products, including non-dairy margarine, that approximate the taste and texture of dairy products. These make it possible to eat meat with creamy sauces and creamy desserts after a meat meal.

To ensure the complete separation of meat and milk, kosher kitchens have separate dishes, pans and washing-up utensils for each. These must be stored separately in the kitchen.

Cheese and Rennet

Natural rennet, the ingredient used to curdle milk for cheese-making, comes from the lining of an animal's stomach. Therefore, the cheese made from it is not kosher. Much modern cheese is made with vegetable rennet and not necessarily labelled as such, but to be sure, one should eat only cheeses that are marked "Suitable for Vegetarians", or that have the appropriate kosher certification marking.

Gelatine in Dairy Products

Because gelatine is made from animal bones, it is not kosher. Kosher gelatine made from seaweed (carrageen), is vegetarian, and must be used instead. Care should be taken with products such as yogurt, as they can often contain gelatine. For this reason, many Jews will eat only milk products that are marked as kosher.

Above: The quality of kosher wines has improved tremendously over the last few years, and an excellent selection is now available.

ALCOHOL

Spirits and grain alcohol are permitted by Kashrut, as is wine, although wine (and wine products such as brandy) carry a few provisos.

Wine must be labelled kosher, which means that the grapes have been harvested and the wine prepared, processed and bottled under rabbinical supervision. In the not-too-distant past kosher wines were barely drinkable; now, however, there are some wonderful dry and deliciously drinkable wines coming out of Israel, California and France. Traditional sweet Kiddush wines are also available.

All kosher wine is kosher for Passover. Grain alcohol, such as whisky, is not permitted at Passover (though vodka is, since it is made from potatoes).

Left (clockwise from top): milk, Cheddar cheese, goat's cheese, curd (farmer's) cheese and yogurt are just a few of the dairy products that can be enjoyed in the kosher kitchen.

KOSHER FOR SHABBAT

"Ye shall kindle no fire throughout your habitations upon the sabbath day" (Exodus 35:3). No fire for domestic use can be lit in religious homes on Shabbat. No stove should be turned on, even if it is electric. A stove may be left on to keep food warm or to cook food very slowly, but it may not be used for actual cooking on Shabbat.

Many rules surround the definition of what precisely constitutes cooking if a warmer or low-heat gadget is used – some say that food must be partially cooked before Shabbat begins. Water must be previously boiled, then kept warm for Shabbat in an urn which must not be turned on or off.

This injunction applies to all holidays and celebrations, in addition to the weekly Shabbat, and has given rise to the many long-cooked dishes featured in Jewish cooking throughout the world such as dafina, cholent, and other bean and meat dishes that require long, slow cooking to make them succulent.

KASHRUT FOR PESACH

In addition to the requirements for the rest of the year, there is a special set of rules that applies to foods during the Passover festival.

During Pesach no leavened foods may be eaten. This means that no bread, breadcrumbs, flour, yeast, baking powder or bicarbonate of soda (baking soda) may be eaten. Cakes must also be eschewed unless they are prepared using special meal made from ground matzo or from potato flour (potato starch). Eggs can be used as a raising agent in cakes, as it is not the fermentation of grains that causes the cake to rise, but rather the air trapped in the beaten egg.

Ashkenazim eschew many vegetables that could be considered grains or ingredients that could be made into breads or cakes. These include green beans, corn, peas, chickpeas, lentils and dried beans. Sephardi Jews, however, eat all vegetables and some eat rice.

Before Pesach begins, the house must be cleared entirely of all leavened foods and ingredients. Many religious Jews simply seal cupboards that contain hametz (leaven) with tape, unsealing them again when the festivities are over.

Beer and other alcoholic drinks made with yeast are forbidden during Pesach, although kosher wine is permitted to carry out the observances and traditions of the festival.

Many Sephardim are careful about the milk and dairy products that they consume during Pesach, and will drink only milk that is marked kosher for Pesach to be sure that it is permissable under the laws of Kashrut.

Both Ashkenazi and Sephardi Observant families have separate sets of dishes, cutlery and pans for exclusive use during Pesach. These are stored away for the rest of the year. To make ordinary kitchenware kosher for Pesach, it must be scalded in boiling water. Even the stove must be koshered – the fire and grill (broiler) heated until red hot – before the stove is considered fit to be cooked on for the holiday.

PAREVE FOODS

In Yiddish, these foods are known as *pareve,* and in Hebrew they are *parva*. These are the neutral foods that are neither meat nor dairy. They do not, therefore, have the same restrictions imposed upon them and can be eaten with either meat or dairy foods.

All plant foods such as vegetables, grains and fruit are pareve, as are eggs and permitted fish. However, if a pareve food is cooked with a fat that is derived from meat (such as chicken fat) or dairy (such as butter or cream), the food is no longer pareve.

Jews who keep kosher will not usually eat pareve foods that have been prepared outside the home, as they could have been prepared using non-kosher fats.

Below (clockwise from top left): Pareve foods such as barley, onions, aubergines (eggplant), tomatoes and eggs can be eaten with either meat or dairy foods.

JEWISH FOODS

The foods of the Jewish table not only have their roots in ritual and tradition, but also reflect the flavours of the countries where Jews have settled. Ashkenazi and Sephardi foods are very different from one another, although cross-cultural marriages and the intermingling of people from different backgrounds have blurred the boundaries. With the myriad Jewish communities coming together again, this is a time in which Jews can feel as well as say "Am Yisrael Chil"
— We are One People.

DAIRY FOODS

In both Ashkenazi and Sephardi kitchens, all dairy foods are held in very high esteem, a tribute to the biblical description of the land of Israel as a "land of milk and honey". There are strict rules concerning the consumption of dairy foods, but they do not have great religious significance except during the festival of Shavuot. This is sometimes known as the dairy festival and is a time when dairy products are enjoyed for main meals, in preference to meat, which is normally enjoyed at festivals and celebrations.

MILK AND DAIRY PRODUCTS

The milk taken from any kosher animal is considered kosher. Cows, goats and sheep are all milked and the milk is then drunk or made into various dairy products such as butter, yogurt and sour cream. The influences of the past can be seen in the dairy products that are enjoyed by Jews today.

Left (clockwise from top left): Cottage cheese, cream cheese, feta cheese and kashkaval are among the many kosher Jewish cheeses.

In the past, in Northern Europe, milk from cows was readily available and, because the weather was cool, spoilage was not a great problem. Many towns and villages had small dairies that produced sour cream, butter, buttermilk, cottage cheese and cream cheese, and families often owned a cow or two of their own. In Lithuania, however, goats tended to be kept more often than cows and were referred to as Jewish cattle. In warmer countries, especially those situated around the Mediterranean, goats and sheep were much easier to raise, and their milk was more suitable for making fermented dairy products such as yogurt, feta cheese and halloumi. Today, Israel is a great producer of yogurts and sour creams.

Left (clockwise from top): Sour cream products such as shoumenet, sour cream and smetana are very popular in the Jewish kitchen.

Cheeses

A wide variety of kosher cheeses are produced in modern-day Israel, including kashkaval, which resembles a mild Cheddar; halloumi; Bin-Gedi, which is similar to Camembert, and Galil, which is modelled on Roquefort. Fresh goat's cheeses are particularly popular in Israel and are of a very good quality.

Cream cheese has been very popular with Ashkenazim since the days of shtetl, where it was made in small, Jewish-owned dairies, and sold in earthenware pots or wrapped in leaves. Soft cheeses such as cream cheese and cottage cheese were also made in the home. Cream cheese is the classic spread for bagels, when it is known as a schmear. It can be flavoured with other ingredients such as chopped spring onions (scallions) and smoked salmon.

Dairy Delis

These were a great legacy of New York's Lower East Side Jewish community. Among the most famous restaurants was Ratners, known for its elderly waiters who were invariably grumpy, nosy, bossy and ultimately endearing. Dairy shops and restaurants sold specialities such as cheese-filled blintzes, cheesecake, cream cheese shmears and knishes. Among other treats were boiled potatoes with sour cream, hot or cold borscht, cheese kugels and noodles with cottage cheese.

E G G S

These represent the mysteries of life and death and are very important in Jewish cuisine. They are brought to a family on the birth of a child, and served after a funeral to remind the mourners that, in the midst of death, we are still embraced by life. They also represent fertility. In some Sephardi communities, an egg will be included as part of a bride's costume, or the young couple will be advised to step over fish roe or eat double-yolked eggs to help increase their fertility.

Eggs are pareve so may be eaten with either meat or dairy foods. They are nutritious and filling and provide a good source of protein when other sources may be lacking or forbidden due to the laws of Kashrut.

EGGS FOR PESACH

These feature prominently in the Pesach Seder (ceremonial meal) – both symbolically and as a food. It is said that a whole egg represents the strength of being a whole people (unbroken, the shell is strong; broken, it is weak).

Eggs are also an important ingredient during Pesach, as raising agents may not be used for baking and eggs, when beaten into a cake mixture, can help the cake to rise.

Making Roasted Eggs

A roasted egg is traditionally placed on the Seder plate to represent the cycle of life. It is not usually eaten.

Place a hard-boiled egg over a gas flame, turning occasionally, until it is lightly browned all over. Alternatively, the egg can be roasted in the oven.

Right: Eggs from any kosher bird are considered kosher, as long as they do not contain any trace of blood.

Making Eggs in Salt Water

This simple dish is the first thing eaten when the Pesach service is over. It is only eaten at this time. Allow about 1½ eggs per person.

1 Hard-boil the eggs. Meanwhile, in a small bowl, dissolve 2.5ml/½ tsp salt in 120ml/4fl oz/½ cup warm water. Cool, then chill.

2 Shell the eggs and serve with the salt water for dipping, or place them in the bowl of salt water.

HAMINADOS EGGS

These are a Sephardi speciality. Whole eggs are cooked very slowly with onion skins or coffee grounds, to colour the shells. Alternatively, they may be added to the slow-cooked stew, dafina. They are delicious mashed with leftover cholent, in savoury pastries or chopped and added to simmered brown broad (fava) beans with a little garlic, onion, olive oil and hot chilli sauce.

Making Haminados Eggs

Cooking the eggs with onion skins colours the egg shells but does not impart any flavour to the egg inside.

1 Place 12 whole eggs in a pan and add 5ml/1 tsp each of salt and pepper. Drop in the brown outer skins from 8–10 onions, pour over water to cover and 90ml/6 tbsp olive oil.

2 Bring to the boil, then lower the heat to very low and cook for 6 hours, adding more water as needed. Shell and serve.

> **Classic Deli Dishes**
> Hard-boiled egg, chopped with onion and mixed with a little chicken fat or mayonnaise is one of the oldest Jewish dishes. In modern-day Israel, an avocado is often mashed with the eggs. Scrambled eggs with browned onion and shredded smoked chicken on rye toast or bagels make a perfect brunch.

MEAT

For Observant Jews, meat must be kosher. Originally, any Jew versed in the ritual could slaughter meat, but this changed in the 13th century, with the appointment of shochets (ritual slaughterers). To qualify for this post, a man needed to be very learned, pious and upstanding.

Meat has always been an expensive but highly prized item on the Jewish table. For Ashkenazim, it was made even more costly with the levying of a hefty government tax (korobka). This, together with a community tax for Jewish charities, brought the price to twice that for non-kosher meat. None of this deterred Jews from eating meat, however; they simply saved it for Shabbat and other special occasions.

LAMB AND MUTTON

These were favoured by the Sephardim from North Africa and other Arabic lands until the early 20th century, when the strong French influence introduced beef and veal to their table. Due to the time-consuming removal of the sciatic nerve required by the laws of Kashrut, the Ashkenazim avoided eating the hindquarters of lamb and mutton until the 15th century when a meat shortage made the lengthy procedure worthwhile.

BEEF

This is very popular, especially among European Jews. Brisket is grainy and rough textured, but yields a wonderful flavour when cooked for a long time. The same applies to the short ribs and the chuck or bola. Many of these cuts are not only excellent for pot-roasting and soups; they also make good salt or corned beef and pastrami. Beef shin makes a marvellous soup.

Sausages and Salami

Both Ashkenazim and Sephardim use beef to make a wide array of sausages and salamis. The Ashkenazim tend to favour tasty cured sausages such as frankfurters, knockwurst, knobblewurst and spicy dried sausages while the Sephardim favour fresh sausages, such as the spicy merguez from North Africa and France.

VEAL

This is a favourite meat for all Jewish communities, because it is so delicate and light: shoulder roast, breast of veal, shank and rib chops are all popular cuts along with minced (ground) veal. The breast was often stuffed, then braised with vegetables; minced veal was made into cutlets and meatballs; and, in Vienna, slices of shoulder were pounded until very thin, then lightly coated in breadcrumbs and fried to make crisp, golden schnitzel.

OTHER MEATS

These include goat and deer (venison). Goat is popular in Sephardi cooking and is often used in dishes where lamb could be used such as spicy stews, curries and meatballs. Venison is cooked in similar ways to beef.

OFFAL

Historically, poorer families tended to eat cheaper cuts of meat such as feet, spleen, lungs, intestines, liver, tongue and brains. These were popular with both Ashkenazim and Sephardim, especially Yemenite Jews who are still famed for their spicy offal soups.

COOKING KOSHER MEAT

Kosher meat is usually tough because the cuts eaten tend to contain a high proportion of muscle, the meat is not tenderized by being hung but must be butchered within 72 hours of slaughter, and because the salting of meat to remove blood produces a dry result.

Because of this, meat is generally cooked slowly by stewing, braising, pot-roasting and simmering until the meat is tender. These long, slow methods are also ideal for the Shabbat meal, which can be prepared and cooked ahead of time, then left in the oven to grow beautifully tender.

Above: Veal escalopes (US scallops) are often pounded to make the classic Viennese schnitzel.

When meat is cooked quickly, for instance kebabs, the meat is marinated first to tenderize it. Chopping or mincing (grinding) meat has a similar effect, which is why so many Jewish meat recipes are for meatballs, patties and meat loaves. These dishes also allow a modest amount of meat to be stretched.

Meatballs in Many Guises
Spiced or seasoned meatballs are popular throughout the Jewish world and come in many forms.
• Russian bitkis are made from minced (ground) beef, often with chopped onion, and may be fried, grilled (broiled) or simmered, often alongside a chicken for a Shabbat or other festive meal.
• Kotleta are flattened meatballs that are fried.
• Cylindrical Romanian mitetetlai are flavoured with garlic, often with parsley, and are fried or grilled (broiled) until brown.
• The Sephardi world has myriad meatballs: albondigas, boulettes, kefta or kofta, and yullikas. They are highly spiced and can be grilled (broiled), cooked over an open fire or simmered in sauces.

Traditional Flavourings

Each region favours certain flavourings. The Polish choose sweet-and-sour flavours; the Germans sweet and fruity; the Russians savoury, with onions; the Lithuanians peppery. Sephardim favour spices and vegetables. Moroccans add sweet, fruity flavours; Tunisians prefer sharp spices; Turkish Jews add tomatoes and fresh herbs such as dill; Persians prefer delicate flavours, with herbs, fruits and vegetables and beans.

Making Meatloaf

A traditional Ashkenazi dish, meatloaf is called klops. Serve hot or cold.

1 Preheat the oven to 180°C/350°F/ Gas 4. In a bowl, combine 800g/1¾lb minced (ground) meat, 2 grated onions, 5 chopped garlic cloves, 1 shredded carrot, chopped parsley, 60ml/4 tbsp dried breadcrumbs, 45–60ml/3–4 tbsp tomato ketchup and 1 beaten egg.

2 Form the mixture into a loaf and place in a roasting pan. Spread 60ml/ 4 tbsp tomato ketchup over the surface, arrange 2 sliced tomatoes on top, then sprinkle over 2–3 sliced onions.

3 Cover the pan with foil and bake for 1 hour. Remove the foil, increase the temperature to 200°C/400°F/Gas 6 and remove some of the onions. Bake for a further 15 minutes, or until the meat is cooked and the onions are browned.

Making Calf's Foot Jelly

This light, richly flavoured aspic, known as petcha, is a traditional Ashkenazi dish. Serve as an appetizer with slices of hard-boiled egg.

1 Cut 4 cleaned calf's feet into pieces, and place in a large pan. Pour over cold water to cover. Bring to the boil, then simmer for 5 minutes. Drain and rinse the feet well in cold water.

2 Place the feet in a clean pan and add 500g/1¼lb veal shin, 1–2 halved onions, 1 halved carrot, 1 chopped celery stick, several sprigs of parsley, thyme and rosemary, 2 bay leaves, 8–10 garlic cloves, and 7.5ml/1½ tsp salt and 30ml/2 tbsp whole black peppercorns. Pour over enough cold water to cover.

3 Bring the mixture to the boil, then simmer for about 5 minutes, skimming off any scum that rises to the surface. Simmer for a further 4 hours, skimming the surface occasionally.

4 Remove the calf's feet from the pan with a slotted spoon and set aside. Strain the stock into a large bowl and stir in 30ml/2 tbsp lemon juice.

5 Remove the meat from the bones, cut into bitesize pieces and add to the stock. Chill until set, then serve.

Meats from the Deli Counter

Traditionally, Jewish delis sold either meat or dairy foods, never both. Meat delis always have a wonderful choice of cured meats and sausages – salt beef on rye, thin slices of salami, smoky pastrami or frankfurters and knockwurst with a generous helping of sauerkraut. There are cooked meats too, such as boiled brisket with a rich, brown gravy and boiled flanken, ready to eat with a little dab of hot mustard.

Right: Beef salami, salt beef and spicy pastrami are classic deli fare.

POULTRY

This is considered meat in the laws of Kashrut, and is therefore subject to all the same rules as regards slaughter and preparation. Any part of a permitted bird can be eaten.

CHICKEN

This is probably the most popular fowl for both Sephardim and Ashkenazim. Like beef and lamb, chicken was once reserved for the Shabbat or other festive meal. However, chicken was usually served more frequently as people often raised a few chickens of their own and could take them to the shochet when the time came.

Chicken is often first simmered in water or stock to make soup, then roasted for a main course. There is no more potent an image of Jewish cooking than a bowl of steaming hot chicken soup with noodles or dumplings. It has always been considered very nourishing. Moses Maimonides, the Jewish philosopher and doctor, touted its benefits in the 12th century, and in recent years, scientific studies have confirmed its value, proving the aptness of its nickname – Jewish penicillin. Chicken backs are rich with morsels of meat and are excellent for soup; as are the feet and wings.

Meatballs made from minced (ground) chicken were a favourite food of Persian and Turkish Jews, especially when simmered along with aubergine (eggplant). Iraqis were famous for their spiced chicken croquettes, which they introduced to India and Burma. Indian Jews cook marvellous chicken curries, substituting coconut milk for yogurt, which is not permitted with chicken. A favourite Sephardi dish, eaten on the streets of Jerusalem, consists of chicken giblets and livers, grilled (broiled) until brown and crisp, and eaten with pitta bread and a hot, spicy pepper sauce.

OTHER BIRDS

Turkey, duck, goose and farmed pigeon (US squab), quail and poussin are also eaten. In Morocco, it is traditional for bridal couples to be served pigeons cooked with sweet fruits on their wedding night, to grant them a sweet life together.

In the Sephardi tradition, birds were often stuffed with couscous, spicy meat, rice and dried fruit, or with herbs and milder spices such as cinnamon. The Sephardim also liked stewed poultry with quinces or pomegranates, or flavoured with tomatoes, (bell) peppers, chickpeas or olives.

The art of raising geese for foie gras was acquired by Jews in Ancient Egypt, and it is believed that it was they who introduced the delicacy to France. In the Ashkenazi tradition, poultry necks are often stuffed with a mixture of chopped liver or kishke (stuffed derma) stuffing to make a sausage known as a helzel.

Left: Chicken is used in an array of classic Jewish dishes from chicken soup to schnitzel.

SCHMALTZ AND GREBENES

Rendered chicken fat (schmaltz), and the crisp morsels of skin left over after the rendering (grebenes), are widely used in Jewish cooking. Schmaltz was long considered a symbol of abundance and there is a traditional Yiddish saying: "He's so lucky that even when he falls, he falls right into a schmaltz bucket!" Spread schmaltz on bread with onions or use it to flavour cholent or to make chopped liver.

Making Schmaltz and Grebenes

One chicken won't make very much schmaltz, so save the fat and skin from several chickens and chill or freeze until you have 450g/1lb.

1 Using a sharp knife, cut the fat and skin into small pieces. Place in a large, heavy pan and pour over water to cover. Bring to the boil and cook over a high heat until the water has evaporated.

2 Reduce the heat and add about 2½ chopped onions and 1–2 whole garlic cloves. Cook over a medium heat, removing the garlic when golden.

3 When all the fat has been rendered and the grebenes are crunchy, remove the grebenes with a slotted spoon.

FISH

Permitted fish are classified as pareve, so have no restrictions with regard to combining with other foods. Its versatility makes fish very important on the Jewish table. It may hold centre stage, as when a whole fish is served at Rosh Hashanah, but more often it is served as an appetizer or one of several dishes on a buffet table.

From the fresh fish counter, there is a wide choice. Sea bass, cod, sole and flounder, haddock, hake and mackerel are all popular sea fish, with perch, pike and trout among the best-loved of the freshwater varieties.

Some fish are thought of as being more Jewish than others. However, this apparent preference for certain fish has simply come about because of geography and traditional availability. Carp is a particular favourite among Ashkenazi Jews, as is pike. Carp was brought to Europe by Jews who encountered it in China when involved in the silk trade in the 15th century, while pike was introduced into the USA from Germany in the 19th century and grew in popularity as waves of Jewish immigrants arrived in the country.

Making Jellied Carp

This traditional, and delicious, dish of poached carp in jelly is a legacy of the Jews of Eastern Europe.

1 Cut 1kg/2¼lb prepared fresh carp into 8–10 slices. Heat 15ml/1 tbsp vegetable oil in a large pan. Add about 2½ chopped onions and sauté until golden brown.

2 Add 2–3 bay leaves, 1–2 parsley and thyme sprigs, 1–2 lemon slices and the carp to the pan and season well with salt and black pepper.

Above: Carp is one of the fish traditionally enjoyed by Ashkenazi Jews. It is used to make such classic dishes as gefilte fish and jellied carp.

3 Pour 450ml/¾ pint/scant 2 cups hot fish stock and 250ml/8fl oz/1 cup dry white wine into the pan. Bring to the boil, then simmer for 1 hour until the fish is tender. Cool slightly, then remove the carp and pack it into a mould.

4 Strain the stock into a large bowl. Dissolve 2 sachets kosher gelatine in 150ml/¼ pint/⅔ cup of the stock, then stir into the remaining stock. Pour over the fish and chill until firm. Serve with lemon wedges and horseradish.

Fish from the Deli Counter

No Ashkenazi celebration is complete without some kind of fish from the deli counter. A good deli will smell deliciously of smoked and cured fish. The art of preserving fish is very much a speciality of the Ashkenazi Jews. They perfected the technique so that stocks of fish could be laid down to last all year. Methods used included salting, brining, smoking and marinating.

In a good deli you will find silky smoked salmon (lox), its natural orange colour providing a contrast to the smoked whitefish in its shimmering gold skin. In addition there will be salt herring, smoked herring, pickled herring, herring in sour cream, herring in brine and herring salad. Carp, smoked and seasoned with paprika, is known as sable and is a rare treat. It is sold only in the most traditional delis. You will find also gefilte fish in the deli, either freshly made or in jars, the liquid jellied and flavoured sweetly in the Polish manner, or peppery, in the Russian or Lithuanian tradition.

Below: Spicy, piquant pickled herring rollmops and thinly sliced smoked salmon are perfect for a Shabbat brunch.

GRAINS, BEANS AND LENTILS

For Jews, grains, beans, peas and lentils have long been the staff of life and have fuelled generations. In many places, a certain type of grain or pulse (legume) actually helped to define the cuisine of the community. In Romania it was mamaliga, a corn meal porridge that resembles polenta; in North Africa it was couscous; and for many places in the East, the staple food was rice. In Russia, Poland and Ukraine, kasha (buckwheat) was widely eaten. Pulses are added to cholent, hamim and dafina, the slow-cooked stews that are traditionally served for Shabbat.

KASHA

This nutty, earthy grain is the partially milled grain or groat of buckwheat. It is traditionally used in Ashkenazi cooking and is very evocative for Ashkenazim who grew up eating it.

Kasha is traditionally served with roasts and pot-roasts, bathed in gravy and meat juices, or may be used as a filling for knishes and dumplings. It can also be combined with onions, wild mushrooms and noodles. Kasha varnishkes, a classic Ashkenazi dish of kasha, butterfly-shaped noodles and onions, is traditionally eaten at the festival of Purim.

Making Kasha

The grains may be fine, medium or coarse. Kasha should be toasted before being cooked, to keep it from going mushy and give it a nutty flavour. It is often toasted with egg before being simmered, to keep the grains separate.

To toast kasha, heat in a heavy pan over a medium heat for a few minutes until the grains start to give off their aroma. Add stock, bring to the boil, reduce the heat and cover. Simmer gently for 10–20 minutes until tender.

To toast kasha with egg, combine about 250g/9oz/1¼ cups kasha in a bowl with 1 beaten egg. Add the mixture to a cold heavy pan. Stir well, then turn on the heat to medium-high. Stir constantly while the grains toast and the egg sets. When the grains look dry, add stock or water and cook the kasha as above.

MAMALIGA

This golden corn meal is widely used in Eastern Europe and is Romania's national dish. It resembles polenta and can be eaten either soft and porridge-like, or spread out on a tray and left to chill until firm, then sliced and fried or grilled (broiled). It is good hot or cold.

Mamaliga is eaten by everyone in Romania, whether Jewish or not. For breakfast, it is drizzled with honey or jam and served with sour cream; for lunch it is topped with cottage cheese or Brinza, a cheese similar to feta, and butter. It tastes great with roasted (bell) peppers and tomatoes, or for a meat meal, with a pot-roast and gravy, or grilled beef patties or sausages.

Making Mamaliga

The corn meal used for mamaliga, like that for polenta, may have small or large grains, so the cooking time will need to be adjusted accordingly. To make mamaliga for a dairy meal, stir in a few tablespoons of butter and about 450g/1lb/2 cups cottage cheese or Brinza and serve hot.

1 Put 300g/11oz/2¾ cups golden corn meal or polenta in a bowl with 15ml/ 1 tsp salt. Pour in about 250ml/8fl oz/ 1 cup cold water, stir well and leave to stand for a few minutes. Meanwhile, bring 900ml/1½ pints/3¾ cups water to the boil.

2 Gradually add the corn meal to the boiling water, stirring constantly. Cook over a low heat for 20–35 minutes, stirring, until all the water has been absorbed. If it sticks to the pan, add more water and stir vigorously.

Left (clockwise from top left): Pareve grains such as barley, kasha (buckwheat) and bulgur wheat are important staples in both Ashkenazi and Sephardi kitchens.

Grilling Mamaliga

Pour the hot, freshly cooked corn meal on to a buttered or oiled sheet or platter and spread it out to a thickness of about 2.5–4cm/1–1½in. Leave to cool, then cut the mamaliga into fingers, brush with oil and grill (broil). Top with grated cheese, tomatoes or mushrooms.

BARLEY

This high-protein food is a good source of B vitamins. It is an indispensable ingredient in Eastern European dishes such as mushroom and barley soup, or barley with vegetables and butter (lima) beans. A small amount of meat is sometimes added.

BULGUR WHEAT

This is the partially milled grain of the whole wheat and is widely used in the Middle East. It comes in different sizes, from small and fine through to large. Bulgur wheat is sometimes eaten in place of couscous or rice, with savoury stews or soups.

COUSCOUS

This grain-like staple actually consists of tiny pellets of pasta, though it is usually categorized as a grain. It has always been very popular with the Jews of North Africa and, when they came to Israel, they brought it with them, in various different sizes. It is easy to

Right: Israeli couscous has much larger grains than regular couscous.

Right (clockwise from top right): Beans, split peas and lentils are rich in protein and can be added to stews to eke out a small amount of meat.

prepare and is usually steamed over a light and savoury spicy stew of vegetables, meats, fish or fruit. Many different types of couscous are available and they are cooked in different ways. Ordinary couscous is first moistened with cold water and left to plump up. It is then steamed over a stew. Fast-cooking couscous usually only needs to be combined with boiling water, then heated through or left to soak.

Israeli couscous, a pea-sized toasted pasta that has become a fashionable ingredient in Europe and America, is cooked in the same way as pasta. It gives a succulent result and is very good in soups and fish dishes.

RICE

This is widely eaten by Jews throughout the world. Chelou is a classic dish of the Persian Jews. As it cooks, the rice at the base of the pan is allowed to form a crisp crust (*tahdeeg*), which is then stirred into the tender rice, providing a tasty contrast of textures. Sometimes, thinly sliced potatoes are also added. Many Iranian Jewish specialities use chelou as their base, topping it with herby vegetable or meat stews. At Rosh Hashanah, Iranian Jews particularly favour rice. The many tiny grains of rice represent the many grains of happiness that are hoped for during the coming year.

CHICKPEAS

These are eaten in great quantities by Sephardi Jews, and Eastern European Jews serve them to celebrate a Brit Milah. They are milled into flour and used as a thickener by Indian and Middle Eastern Jews, and are soaked and ground to make falafel, which is considered by many to be Israel's national dish.

DRIED BEANS AND PEAS

Broad (fava) beans and black-eyed beans (peas) are very popular with the Sephardim. Broad beans are very ancient and have been found at pre-pottery Neolithic B levels in Jericho. Black-eyed beans originated in Ethiopia about four thousand years ago and were recorded in Judea about 1500 BCE (BC). Both are eaten in soups and stews. Dried broad beans are cooked and eaten with garlic, olive oil, hard-boiled eggs and a little tahini.

LENTILS

All types of lentil are made into soup, from split red lentils, which cook quickly, to the superior tasting brown variety. Yellow and green split peas are also popular. In Genesis, the story is told of how Esau sold his birthright for a pottage of lentils.

VEGETABLES

Many vegetables have particular significance in celebrations to mark religious festivals. At Rosh Hashanah, pumpkin may be served; its golden colour signifying prosperity. Green vegetables will be on the table too, symbolizing renewal and happiness, while dried beans and peas signify abundance. Carrots for Rosh Hashanah are cooked in honey to signify a sweet new year. In contrast, at the Pesach Seder, bitter herbs are eaten as a reminder of the bitterness of slavery. At the same time, Ashkenazim eat broad (fava) beans, since this was what the Israelite slaves were fed during their captivity in Egypt. When Ashkenazim celebrate Chanukkah, they do so with potato latkes.

Seven different types of vegetable are used by North African Jews to make one of their specialities, a soup, which represents the seven days of Creation, with Shabbat being the seventh day.

Every year, the new season's produce is eagerly anticipated, and as each vegetable is tasted for the first time, it is customary to recite the Shehehayanu, a prayer of thanksgiving.

Below: Root vegetables such as carrots, turnips and beetroot (beets) are Ashkenazi staples.

THE ASHKENAZI TRADITION

Years of struggle and poverty, when Eastern European Jews were hounded from place to place, and taxed to the limit, made them increasingly inventive as to how they prepared vegetables. Carrots, cabbages, beetroot (beets), onions and turnips may have been dull and heavy but the Jews favoured their strong flavours. They frequently pickled vegetables to improve their taste, and to preserve them through the long winters. Sauerkraut, pickled cucumbers and borscht all date from this era.

When Ashkenazi Jews from Poland and Russia migrated south, they discovered a wealth of new vegetables. Peppers soon became popular, partly because they pickled well, and could be dried to make paprika. Potatoes were eaten with great gusto because they were so tasty and filling, and aubergines (eggplant), which had made their way to Romania from Spain and Italy, became widely used. Tomatoes were not widely accepted for some time, as their red colour was the same hue as blood and there was some question as to whether or not they were kosher – which may account for the Ashkenazi speciality, pickled green tomatoes.

Making Vegetable Eingemachts

Ashkenazim often made sweetmeats from vegetables. Eingemachts is a sweet preserve made from beetroot (beets), which is traditionally eaten at Pesach. It is usually eaten with a spoon along with a hot cup of tea.

1 Put 300g/11oz/scant 1½ cups granulated sugar and 250ml/8fl oz/ 1 cup honey in a large non-reactive pan and stir to combine. Stir in 20ml/4 tsp ground ginger and 120ml/4fl oz/½ cup water. Bring the mixture to the boil, then simmer, stirring occasionally, until the sugar has dissolved.

2 Peel 1.3kg/3lb boiled fresh beetroot, then grate or cut into very thin strips. Thinly slice 3 whole lemons and remove the seeds. Add the beetroot and lemons to the pan and bring to the boil, then lower the heat slightly and cook for 30–40 minutes, or until the mixture is very thick, shaking the pan occasionally.

3 Stir 90g/3½oz/scant 1 cup chopped blanched almonds into the beetroot mixture, then spoon into hot sterilized jars. Cool, then seal. Store in the refrigerator for 2–3 weeks.

Salad Vegetables

In the early days, raw vegetables and salads were not greatly appreciated by Ashkenazim raised in cold climates, where warming, filling stews were a necessity. However, radishes of several kinds were still enjoyed, along with raw turnips, cucumbers, raw onions and garlic. The young spring shoots of garlic were much prized, and were often eaten with dense black bread. Sometimes raw carrots were grated and eaten in salads, as were the young leaves of wild greens and herbs, although these were often cooked and eaten hot as well.

THE SEPHARDI TRADITION

The Jews of the Iberian Peninsula had a much greater variety of fresh vegetables available to them than their northern neighbours. They were among the first Europeans to encounter corn, (bell) peppers, tomatoes and green beans, which were introduced from the New World, and they embraced them with enthusiasm. Jewish merchants helped to popularize these new vegetables by introducing them to the more remote parts of Spain and then, after their expulsion in 1492, to the wider world.

Right: Colourful warm weather vegetables such as (bell) peppers, globe artichokes and aubergines (eggplant) form the basis of many Sephardi dishes.

Globe artichokes and pumpkins were reputedly brought to Italy by the Jews. So too were aubergines (eggplant), which were much valued for their meaty texture, particularly when meat itself was not available, or had to be omitted because of the presence of dairy foods.

Sephardi Jews have always been known for their love of vegetables. They add vegetables to stews, pilaffs and soups. Because they cook with olive oil, vegetable dishes are pareve so they may be served with meat or dairy.

They are cooked simply, then dressed with olive oil and lemon juice. Vegetables are also perfect partners for eggs. Sephardi specialities range from the North African turmeric-tinted potato omelette, a variation on tortilla, to the Sicilian spinach tortino and a Spanish-Syrian dish of aubergine with eggs and cheese. The repertoire also includes chakshouka, a delicious Arabian dish consisting of (bell) peppers, tomatoes and eggs.

From the Deli Counter

Potato salad, coleslaw, cucumber and onions, Russian salad, roasted (bell) peppers, Romanian aubergine (eggplant) salad and marinated mixed vegetables are just some of the tasty vegetable offerings that can be found in the deli. Sauerkraut is another deli staple, while dill pickles are the star attraction. American deli kosher dill pickles are not made with added sweetening or vinegar, just brine with spices and so much garlic that you can smell them down the street. More recently, specialities from Israel such as baba ghanoush have become popular.

Left: Tubs of coleslaw, dill pickles and potato salad are just a few of the delectable offerings found in the deli.

FRUITS, NUTS AND SEEDS

Since the Garden of Eden when Eve ate the proverbial apple, fruit has always been very important to the Jewish table. The first fruits of every season are the subject of specific blessings, with special affection being reserved for melons, figs, dates and grapes, because of their prominent place in the Bible. Nuts and seeds are also widely eaten, providing valuable protein and variety to many dishes.

FRUITS

All fresh fruits are considered kosher and, for some very strict Jews, it is the only food they will eat if they are not sure of the Kashrut of a kitchen. Fresh fruit can be eaten whole, uncut by treyf (not kosher) knives. There is no need for a plate or cooking pan, which might be treyf.

Israel is one of the world's leading fruit growers. Jaffa oranges, juicy grapefruit, kumquats and tiny lime- and lemonquats are grown for local consumption and export, alongside persimmons (Sharon fruit) from the Sharon valley and delicious avocados.

Below: Apples, plums and cherries are fruits of the Ashkenazi table.

Traditions

At Sukkot a lulav (citron) is used for making the blessings over the sukkah. At Rosh Hashanah, apples are dipped in honey, pomegranates are eaten to celebrate fertility and abundance, quinces are baked and preserved and challah often contains dried fruit.

Ashkenazim make charoset, the fruit and nut paste enjoyed at Pesach, from apples and walnuts, while Sephardim favour tropical fruits and dried fruits.

At Tu b'Shevat, Jews taste their way through a variety of orchard fruit, and at Chanukkah, apple sauce is served with potato latkes.

Regional Specialities

Sephardim, living in lush, warm climates, have always enjoyed a wide variety of fruits including figs, dates, melons and citrus fruits. Quinces are traditionally made into sweet preserves for Rosh Hashanah, stuffed for Sukkot, candied for Pesach, and added to meat stews at other times. Another speciality of the Sephardi Jews, particularly those from North Africa, are preserved lemons that have been pickled in brine. They are often added to savoury dishes such as spicy meat stews.

Fruit was not as easily available to the Ashkenazim and soft and deciduous fruits were a seasonal delight for them. Raspberries, gooseberries, currants, cherries, plums, pears and apples were enjoyed in many dishes from pancakes and pastries to fruit soups, cakes and compotes. Baked apples filled with brown sugar and cinnamon are one of the classics of the Ashkenazi kitchen.

Surplus harvest was often dried or preserved and enjoyed during the rest of the year when the fruits were out of season. Compotes made of dried fruit are still very popular in the Ashkenazi kitchen. Dried fruit is used in cakes and strudels and is often added to meat dishes. Raisins are often added to meatballs and pie fillings, and the classic tzimmes (a savoury meat or vegetable stew) is enriched with dried apricots and prunes.

Below: Quinces, dates and figs are among the warm weather fruits of the Sephardi table.

Making Fruit Soup

Classic Ashkenazi fruit soup makes a refreshing start or end to a meal. Plums, cherries or red berries give a good result, but any fruit can be used.

1 Chop 1.3kg/3lb fruit and place in a large non-reactive pan. Add 1 litre/ 1¾ pints/4 cups water, 475ml/16fl oz/ 2 cups dry white or red wine and the juice of 1 lemon. Stir in a little sugar, honey and cinnamon. Bring to the boil, then simmer until the fruit is tender.

2 Mix 10ml/2 tsp arrowroot with 15ml/1 tbsp cold water. Stir into the soup; bring to the boil and cook, stirring constantly, until thickened.

3 Remove the pan from the heat, stir in a little more water or wine if the soup seems too thick, then stir in a dash of vanilla essence (extract). If using peaches, cherries or apricots, add almond essence instead. Cool, then chill. Serve with sour cream or yogurt.

VARIATION

To make kissel, purée the soup mixture, then press through a strainer into a bowl. Serve chilled, with a drizzle of cream.

NUTS AND SEEDS

These are pareve and enjoyed by both Ashkenazim and Sephardim. They may be added to sweet or savoury dishes as an ingredient or eaten on their own as a snack. Street stalls in Israeli cities sell toasted nuts and seeds, known as garinim, for nibbling.

Almonds are used in sweet and savoury dishes. Mandelbrot (hard almond cookies) are among the classic sweets of the Askenazi kitchen, whereas almond paste is a favourite filling used in the delicate filo pastries of North Africa and Mediterranean countries.

Coconut is used for making macaroons to serve at Pesach. In India, coconut milk is used to give meat curries a creamy quality without the need for yogurt or other dairy foods.

Pistachio nuts are enjoyed throughout the Middle East. Toasted and salted, they are a favourite snack. Unsalted pistachio nuts are crushed and layered into sweet desserts such as baklava, cake fillings and cookies.

Poppy seeds are particularly popular in the Ashkenazi kitchen. They are eaten in cakes such as the classic Russian mohn torte and sprinkled on top of breads such as bagels. Their flavour is intensified when they are roasted and ground to a paste, to be used as a filling for cakes and pastries.

Below: Almonds, sesame seeds and poppy seeds are widely used in Jewish cooking.

Treats from the Deli

The sweet aroma of baked apples welcomes visitors to the deli. Fruit compotes and jellies, and rice puddings studded with dried fruit are all available. Apricot leather – a paste of cooked apricots, dried in sheets or strips, and eaten as a confection or warmed with boiling water until it reverts to a thick paste – is also a deli speciality. Dates are coated with coconut or stuffed with nuts and sold in blocks. Delis with a large Middle Eastern clientele have jars of sweet preserves, ready to be spooned out and eaten with plain cake. Green walnuts, cherries, plums and kumquats are stewed in honey and sold in this way.

Sesame seeds can be purchased whole or hulled, raw or toasted. For optimum flavour, buy raw hulled seeds. Just before use, toast them in a heavy, ungreased pan until fragrant and golden. Toasted sesame seeds can be crushed to make halva or tahini, or simmered with honey or sugar to make sumsum, crisp confections that are sold as street food in Israel.

Walnuts are widely used in Ashkenazi cooking and are an essential ingredient in charoset.

HERBS, SPICES AND FLAVOURINGS

The Ashkenazim used the flavourings of Eastern Europe to create their robust and often piquant dishes, while the Sephardim used their own local flavourings to create a cuisine that is richly spiced and aromatic.

HERBS AND SPICES

A special place is reserved for herbs and spices in the rituals of the Jewish table. Both mild and bitter herbs are eaten at Pesach, while the sweet aroma of cinnamon, ginger, nutmeg and cloves is inhaled as part of the havdalah ceremony that signifies the end of Shabbat, the smell of the spices welcoming the week ahead.

Ashkenazim adopted the flavours of Eastern European cooking: young dill fronds, parsley, spring onions (scallions) and tender young garlic. Spices were

Karpas and Moror

These are the herbs that feature at Pesach. Karpas is the mild herb eaten at the Seder meal. It might be leaves of young lettuce, as favoured in the Sephardi tradition, or parsley, as favoured by the Ashkenazim. Moror are the bitter herbs, eaten as a reminder of the tears shed by Hebrew slaves in Egypt. Grated horseradish is often used, or the bitter greens might be represented by chicory (Belgian endive) or watercress.

added to cakes and breads and occasionally meat dishes. A mixture of herbs and spices was used in pickled vegetables, meats and fish, contributing to their piquant flavours.

Countries with a strong German and Russian heritage introduced Jewish settlers to mustards of various kinds. In delis today you will find a large selection of mustards, such as wholegrain, smooth, sweet and herbed, ready to add their flavour to all manner of Ashkenazi dishes. In Hungary, Ashkenazi Jews encountered paprika, and soon embraced it, making their own versions of dishes dominated by this warm, yet subtle, spice, such as chicken paprikash and meat goulash.

In the same eclectic fashion, Jews embraced other flavours typical of the lands in which they lived: thyme and oregano from the Mediterranean region; cumin and coriander from India; cinnamon and harissa from North Africa and chillies from Mexico.

On the wondrous palette of Middle Eastern cooking, spice mixtures are the culinary colours. They add fragrance and flavour to whatever they touch. Middle Eastern spice blends are many and varied and may be dry ground mixtures or wet pastes made with fresh chillies, garlic and herbs.

Spice blends taste much more intense if they are made from freshly roasted and ground spices.

Above (clockwise from top): Cumin and coriander seeds are favoured in the North African kitchen, while paprika is essential in Hungarian Jewish cooking.

Making Harissa

This hot, spicy paste is used extensively in Tunisian and other North African cooking. It is based on medium-sized chillies with a medium hot flavour. The blend is widely sold in jars, but it is easy to make your own.

1 Put 10–15 whole dried chillies in a pan with water to cover. Bring to the boil, then remove from the heat.

2 When the chillies are cool enough to handle, remove the stems, seeds and membrane, then pound to a purée with 10 garlic cloves, 5ml/1 tsp each of ground coriander, caraway and cumin in a mortar with a pestle. Add 2.5ml/½ tsp salt and about 15ml/1 tbsp extra virgin olive oil. Stir in enough cold water to make a thick paste.

Right: Fresh dill is used extensively in Ashkenazi cooking and its aroma is redolent of many classic dishes from the Old Country.

Making Hawaij

This wonderfully fragrant mixture of spices comes from Yemen. It is delicious in stews, soups and sauces.

Place 30ml/2 tbsp black peppercorns and 15ml/1 tbsp caraway seeds in a spice grinder, or use a pestle and mortar. Add 10ml/2 tsp each of ground cumin and turmeric, 5ml/1 tsp cardamom seeds and several pinches of saffron threads. Process to a powder and keep in a tightly sealed jar in a cool, dark place.

Making Berbere

This Ethiopian spice mixture is based on hot chillies.

1 Mix 90g/3½oz paprika with 10ml/ 2 tsp cayenne pepper, the seeds from 20 cardamom pods, 2.5ml/½ tsp ground fenugreek seeds; 1.5ml/¼ tsp each of ground ginger and freshly grated nutmeg, and generous pinches of black pepper, cloves, ground cinnamon and allspice.

2 Lightly toast the mixture in a hot, ungreased pan for less than a minute. When cool, store in a tightly sealed jar.

Making Chermoula

This moist mixture of herbs, spices and aromatics comes from North Africa. It is mainly used as a marinade for fish but is also good with chicken, potatoes and other vegetables.

1 In a bowl, combine 75ml/5 tbsp extra virgin olive oil with 30ml/2 tbsp lemon juice, 4–5 crushed garlic cloves and 10ml/2 tsp ground cumin.

2 Stir 15ml/1 tbsp paprika, 1.5ml/¼ tsp ground ginger and 1 chopped fresh chilli or a pinch of chilli powder into the spice mixture.

3 Add 90ml/6 tbsp chopped fresh coriander (cilantro) leaves and a little flat leaf parsley or mint, if you like, to the bowl, season with salt and mix well or purée to a smooth paste.

Below (clockwise from top left): Rose water, honey and halek are widely used in both sweet and savoury dishes in the Sephardi kitchen.

FLAVOURINGS

There are a number of other flavouring ingredients that play an essential role in Jewish cooking.

Salt is not just used as a seasoning but also plays a role in ritual, especially in kashering. It is seen as a purifying agent and, in biblical times, it was sacrificed at the Temple in Jerusalem. In Morocco, Jews sprinkle salt on newborn babies, to ward off the evil eye. At the Pesach Seder, it is dissolved in water and used to represent the tears of Israelite slaves.

Sour salt (citric acid) is a great favourite in the Ashkenazi kitchen and is used instead of lemon or vinegar to add a sour taste to dishes such as borscht.

Honey has been much loved by Jews since the biblical description of Israel as a land flowing with milk and honey. It is used to represent the sweetness of the year to come at Rosh Hashanah and is also used in baking – most famously in lekach, the Ashkenazi honey cake eaten to celebrate a child's first day at school.

Rose water and orange flower water are fragrant essences used in sweet and savoury dishes. They are added to the syrups poured over sweet pastries, and to savoury tagines and couscous dishes.

Halek, also known as dibis, is a thick date syrup used to flavour sweet and savoury foods. It is readily available in jars, but you can easily make your own. Reconstitute dried dates in water, then boil in a little water until soft. Purée in a food processor, then strain into a clean pan and cook over a medium heat until thickened.

NOODLES, PANCAKES, DUMPLINGS AND SAVOURY PASTRIES

NOODLES

These were once the pride of the Ashkenazi kitchen and housewives were judged on their skills as home-makers (*balaboostas*) by how thin and delicate they could make their noodles. Noodles were cut into a variety of shapes, such as little squares (plaetschen) and small butterflies (varnishkes). Noodles were served in soup, tossed with sour cream or cheese, or layered with other ingredients such as fruit or cheeses and baked into delicious puddings known as kugels. Noodle dough could also be rolled thin and filled to make dumplings, such as the meat-filled kreplach; potato-, kasha- or cabbage-filled pierogi, or cheese- or fruit-filled varenikes.

Noodles were probably introduced to German Ashkenazi kitchens during the 14th century, via the Italian Jews. This was long before they reached the non-Jewish German kitchen during the 16th century. Pasta came to Poland at the same time, possibly through Central Asia, and the Yiddish word for noodles (*lokshen*) comes from the Polish word *lokszyn*. The sauces of the Polish Yiddish kitchen also showed a Central Asian slant. They were based on yogurt, sour cream and fresh cheeses, rather than the rich tomato sauces of Italian extraction. Sephardi cooking showed a more distinctive Italian or Spanish influence as evidenced in kelsonnes, dumplings filled with cheese and eaten at the festival of Shavuot, and calzonicchi, which are filled with spinach and enjoyed for Purim.

Left: Kreplach are meat-filled pasta dumplings that are often enjoyed in chicken soup.

Right: (clockwise from top) Lokshen, farfel, varnishkes and plaetschen are just a few of the classic noodles from the Ashkenazi kitchen.

Making Noodle Dough

Egg noodles are still made at home for special occasions. This is easy to do with a pasta-rolling machine, but they can also be rolled by hand on a well-floured surface with a large rolling pin.

1 Sift 225g/8oz/2 cups plain (all-purpose) flour and 2.5ml/½ tsp salt into a bowl, making a well in the centre.

2 Pour 2 lightly beaten eggs into the flour and mix with a fork, gradually incorporating the eggs into the flour. Continue to stir, using a wooden spoon, until well combined. Alternatively, place all the ingredients in a food processor fitted with the metal blade and mix to form a dough. If the dough is sticky, add a little more flour.

3 Tip the dough on to a floured board and knead until smooth and elastic. Place the dough in a plastic bag, seal and leave for at least 30 minutes.

4 If using a pasta-rolling machine, roll out walnut-size balls of the dough, then, one at a time, feed the dough into the largest opening of the rollers. Fold the flattened dough and repeat, reducing the roller opening until the dough is the desired thickness.

5 If rolling by hand, divide the dough into three equal pieces, then roll out each piece on a floured surface, until it is extremely thin.

Making Noodle Shapes

Lightly sprinkle the sheets of freshly rolled noodle dough with flour, then cut into the desired shape. To cook, drop the pasta into a large pan of boiling salted water and cook for 2–4 minutes.

To make lokshen (flat noodles), roll a sheet of noodle dough into a tight scroll. Using a heavy sharp knife cut the scroll of dough crossways into narrow or wide strips, as desired. Unroll the strips, boil and serve with sauce, in soup or baked with other ingredients in a kugel.

To make plaetschen (little squares), cut a sheet of noodle dough into 1cm/½in squares. Boil and serve in soup.

To make varnishkes (butterflies), cut a sheet of noodle dough into 2.5cm/1in squares. Pinch each square in the centre to form a bow tie or butterfly. Boil and serve in soup or with kasha.

To make farfel (pellets), grate kneaded, unrolled noodle dough through the large holes of a grater to form pellets. Boil and add to soups.

Making Mandlen

These crisp soup garnishes are made from noodle dough. They take their name from the Yiddish word for almond, a reference to their shape and colour.

1 Preheat the oven to 190°C/375°F/Gas 5. Beat 1 egg with 15ml/1 tbsp vegetable oil. Add 2.5ml/½ tsp salt, then mix in about 115g/4oz/1 cup plain (all-purpose) flour until the dough holds together. Knead for 10 minutes. Cover and leave for 20 minutes.

2 Divide the dough into two to four pieces and form each into a rope, about 1cm/½in wide. Cut each one into 1cm/½in pieces and place on an oiled baking sheet. Bake for 35–40 minutes. Alternatively, deep-fry, until just golden.

PANCAKES

Since biblical times pancakes have been popular. In times of plenty, they were made from the finest ingredients and fried in lots of oil. When times were hard, they were made from whatever wild greens and grains could be found and fried in a drop or two of fat.

Pancakes are usually either very thin and filled or thick and crispy. Crêpe-like blintzes are filled with cheese, meat, fruit or vegetables and are often folded into parcels and fried until crisp. Thick, hearty latkes are best known as a treat eaten at Chanukkah, consisting of grated potatoes formed into cakes and fried until golden brown. They can also be enjoyed at any time of year and can be made from spinach, grated apples or a mixture of cottage cheese, matzo meal and eggs. Hearty grains such as kasha can also be used.

Chremslach are thick pancakes eaten at Pesach, made from egg, matzo meal and seasonings. They are good served with a generous spoonful of cooling sour cream or yogurt.

Ataif are Egyptian pancakes, raised with yeast, and served with a sweet syrup and dollops of rich clotted cream. Like other dairy-filled pancakes, they are enjoyed at Shavuot, the festival when dairy products are traditionally eaten in abundance.

Below: Melawah are pancake flat breads eaten by Yemenite Jews, often with chopped tomatoes and spicy zchug.

DUMPLINGS

Generations of Jewish cooks have delighted in dumplings, especially knaidlach made from matzo meal and egg. The word *knaidlach* comes from *knodel,* the German for dumpling. Knaidlach are as much a part of Yiddish cooking as dumplings are of Eastern European peasant food. Because they were made with matzo, knaidlach were eaten for Shabbat and other festivals, especially Pesach, when bread is forbidden.

Different Jewish communities added their distinctive flavour to knaidlach: some added chopped herbs such as parsley or chives, or aromatics such as garlic or grated onions. Others stuffed them with a bit of meat, while the Viennese Jews added a pinch of dried ginger to the mixture. Knaidlach can be big balls or small two-bite wonders and can be tender and light or solid and heavy. Cold cooked knaidlach can be cut into bitesize pieces and browned with eggs and mushrooms.

Sephardi dumplings are made from noodles stuffed with meat, then floated in soup. Alternatively, they may be made from rice as is the case with the Middle Eastern kobeba, meat-filled dumplings much like kibbeh, using rice instead of bulgur wheat.

Below: Knaidlach are the Ashkenazi matzo balls that are traditionally served in chicken soup.

SAVOURY PASTRIES

These are popular with both Ashkenazi and Sephardi Jews. Whenever there was something special to celebrate, the women of the community would gather and spend days preparing pastries.

Ashkenazi Pastries

Classic Ashkenazi pastries include knishes (half-moon shaped turnovers), strudels (wafer-thin pastry rolled around fillings) and piroshkis (small pies). They may be filled with kasha, mashed potatoes and onions, minced (ground) meat, browned cabbage, chopped egg and sometimes smoked salmon. The dough can be shortcrust (unsweetened) pastry or puff pastry, but there are also yeast doughs and even doughs made from mashed potato. The pastries may then be baked or fried.

Above: Kibbeh are classic Sephardi dumplings made of pounded bulgur wheat and minced (ground) meat.

Sephardi Pastries

The Sephardim have a virtually endless number of pastries, with many different types of pastry and filling. They are made in an array of shapes, including cigars, half moons, triangles, rectangles, squares, circles and even cones and round balls, and may be baked or deep-fried in oil.

Borekas are eaten wherever Turkish, Greek and Balkan Jews have settled. These pastries are flaky on the outside, with tender layers within. Borekas can be tiny one-bite pastries or made as tapadas – big trays to cut into individual portions. They are usually filled with aubergine (eggplant) and tomatoes, cheese, spinach or meat.

Iraqi Jews traditionally fill their pastries with mashed chickpeas and chicken. Also from Iraq are sambusaks, crisp shortcrust pastries filled with egg and cheese or vegetables or meat. They are usually topped with sesame seeds or a blend of za'atar herbs containing thyme. Italian Jews fill their savoury burricche with a variety of mixtures, from tuna to liver, and even make sweet pastries with pumpkin and glacé (candied) fruit. Pumpkin pastries are a speciality of Bukharan Jews.

The Spanish and Portuguese Jews have empanadas, crisp little pastries filled with meats, fish or vegetables.

Left: Kaddaif is an unusual, shredded wheat-like pastry that is very popular in the Sephardi kitchen.

Bishak are Bukharan baked pastries made from pizza dough filled with sweet and peppery cooked pumpkin.

Brik are crisp, fried filo pastries, filled with tuna or meat, and a raw egg.

Borekas, sambusak, pasteles and buricche are crisp shortcrust pastries filled with cheese, aubergine (eggplant), and tomato or meat.

Boyos are little pies made from dough layered with mature (sharp) cheese, fried onions and vegetables.

Empanadas are crisp Spanish pastries, usually filled with vegetables and meat. A Turkish version combines fish with crushed walnuts, and an Italian version combines fish and anchovies with chopped parsley.

Filo pastry is a stretched, tissue-paper-thin pastry made from flour and water with a touch of oil for elasticity. It is brushed with oil or butter and rolled around a filling before being fried or baked. Filo pastry is bought ready-made as it requires great skill and years of practice to make it successfully.

Kaddaif is a shredded pastry that looks much like shredded wheat. It is also known as konafa. It is usually used for sweet pastries, which are stuffed with nuts, baked, then soaked in syrup. Like filo dough kaddaif is usually purchased ready-made, as preparing it requires great skill and dexterity.

Khatchapuri are yeast dough pastries filled with cheese from Georgia in Russia. Goat's cheese mixed with Gruyère is a very popular filling, sometimes with a little chopped coriander (cilantro).

Bulemas and rodanchas are made by rolling sheets of filo pastry around a filling, then coiling the rolls on a baking sheet. The dough is very delicate and needs to be handled with great care when being rolled around the filling.

Lamahjeen are small pizza-like pastries made with tomato, tamarind and meat; a speciality of the Jews of Aleppo.

A mina is a Sephardi pie made using soaked matzo as a kind of pastry. They are usually served for Pesach when bread and pastry are forbidden. Minas are often served in Mexico, where they are likened to tortillas.

Warka is similar to filo pastry. It is made by quickly tapping a ball of dough on to a hot surface, leaving behind a thin, wispy layer of tissue-thin pastry, which rapidly becomes crisp.

From the Deli Counter

Sweet noodle kugels may be sold cut into big squares and sold as dessert. Potato latkes can be bought all year round, but are particularly popular at Chanukkah. Blintzes are often sold in delis – hot, freshly cooked blintzes will often be on the menu for brunch, while take-away blintzes can be reheated at home.

Many delis sell hot or cold knishes or piroshkis, ready to eat on the spot or to take home for later, filled with anything from kasha to meat to spinach. Filo pastries can also be found – spinach and cheese is a particularly popular filling. Fresh filo pastry and kaddaif are also sold in delis, especially those with a Middle Eastern influence.

Right: Piroshkis and knishes from the Ashkenazi tradition are particular favourites on the deli counter.

BREADS

The world over, bread is very important to the Jews. A meal without bread is not a meal, according to the dictates of the Jewish religion. Without bread, there can be no hamotzi (blessing over the bread that signals the start of a meal) and neither can there be the Birkat Hamazon (grace that usually concludes a meal). A meal without bread can only really be considered a snack.

ASHKENAZI BREADS

In Jewish bakeries, it is usual for the breads to be pareve – made without butter or milk so that they can be eaten with either meat or dairy foods. There is challah, rye bread, pumpernickel, bagels, Kaiser rolls and onion rolls – the variety is astonishing and, if you happen to have wandered into an ethnic Jewish bakery, you may well encounter some wonderful regional specialities as well as the usual fare.

All ethnic groups have a wide variety of breads, both for everyday use and special occasions. When the Ukrainian Ashkenazim emigrated to America, they brought with them sourdough loaves of seeded rye, dark pumpernickel and onion-crusted

Right: Pumpernickel, from the Ashkenazi tradition, is dark and sour with a crisp crust.

rolls. Walking into one of their bakeries is a joy: the smells of baking – yeast, flour, a whiff of something sweet – mingling with the scent of the wood-burning stove.

Bagels are an Ashkenazi classic that travelled from the shtetls and ghettos of Eastern Europe and are now enjoyed all over the world. They lend themselves to any number of different fillings and are satisfyingly chewy.

Bagels are usually made in bakeries that bake nothing else, because the procedure for making them is a special one. The dough rings are first briefly poached in huge vats of water before being glazed and baked. This technique creates the distinctive dense, chewy texture that has made bagels so popular. To walk past a bagel bakery without venturing in is just about impossible. The alluring smell inevitably entices you in, and you'll want to get yourself a nice hot bagel before setting off once more.

Above: Challah is the traditional bread of Shabbat and festivals and may be braided, round or shaped like a ladder, depending on the festival.

Sweet challah is the traditional Shabbat and festival bread of the Ashkenazi Jews. The dough is made with eggs and vegetable oil, which gives it a soft texture, similar to that of brioche, and is lightly sweetened with honey or sugar.

The loaves are usually braided, made with three, six or even twelve strands of dough. During Rosh Hashanah challah may be shaped into a round or crown, in honour of the Rosh Hashanah blessing: "The whole world will crown thee." On the eve of Yom Kippur, the challah is shaped like a ladder, raised arms or wings, representing prayers rising heavenwards.

Boulkas are small, individual challah rolls, shaped into rounds, braids or spirals and dusted with poppy seeds, that are frequently served at weddings.

SEPHARDI BREADS

These vary greatly and are very different from the breads of the Ashkenazim. Some are risen; some are flat; some, such as melawah, are slightly puffed and fried to a crisp. One Sephardi bread most of us are familiar with is pitta, a flat bread favoured by Jews and Arabs alike, and by many other Middle Easterners as well. Iraqi pitta bread is a particularly large flat bread, which resembles an enormous, thick pancake.

Breads that are especially made for the Sabbath include mouna, lahuhua and kubaneh. A coiled bread from Yemen, kubaneh, is made from a rich yeast dough. It is prepared before the Sabbath begins, then steamed in a very low oven overnight.

Israel produces a marvellous array of breads, from the simple everyday loaf, which is crusty on the outside and beautifully tender inside, to large flat breads, which are used for wrapping around vegetables or meat.

Left: Pitta bread came from the Middle East but is now enjoyed by Ashkenazim, Europeans and Americans alike.

MATZO

This is unleavened bread, made for Pesach, when leavened bread may not be eaten. The flat, brittle sheets are served at the table, and are also ground to make a meal that is transformed into cakes, biscuits and cookies. Matzo meal can be fine or coarse, while matzo farfel is lightly crushed matzo.

For Pesach, matzo is prepared under special guidelines and the packaging is always marked "Kosher for Pesach". Observant Jews often eat schmurah matzo as they are handmade to a very high specification.

Right: Jews eat unleavened matzos at Pesach but they are also enjoyed during the rest of the year.

From the Deli

Oy what sandwiches! A true Jewish deli sandwich is a thing of mammoth proportions. Piles of thinly sliced salami, billows of roasted turkey, peppery pastrami, corned or salt beef, bologna or steamed knockwurst are just some of the possible ingredients, and most likely there will be a combination of several of the above, at least 350g/12oz per sandwich, layered between thick slices of fresh, crusty, tender bread.

A sandwich from one of the legendary New York delis, such as the Carnegie or Second Avenue Deli, Katz's, the Stage Deli or Juniors will be far too thick for the average eater

to get his or her mouth around. It will be necessary to wrap up at least half for later – much, much later.

The Reuben, assumed by many to be a Jewish classic, is not actually kosher. Slices of seeded rye bread contain both corned beef and Swiss cheese – a forbidden combination.

Choosing the filling for your deli sandwich is taxing enough, but it can be even more difficult to decide precisely which bread to have. One thing everyone agrees on, however, is that a sandwich from the deli is never served on sliced white.

Left: A bagel spread generously with cream cheese and topped with wafer-thin slices of smoked salmon is the quintessential Jewish deli snack.

CAKES, PASTRIES AND SWEETMEATS

For Jews, whenever there is something to celebrate, be it a festival or a family occasion, cakes and other sweet treats are very much in evidence. Precisely what is on the table will largely depend on whether the hosts come from the Ashkenazi or Sephardi traditions, as these take very different approaches when it comes to baking.

During Pesach, the kosher kitchens of both Ashkenazim and Sephardim undergo a transformation. At this time, all food must be free of leaven, and eggs are used as the main raising agent instead. The result is a wealth of featherlight sponge cakes, often made with matzo meal and ground nuts.

THE ASHKENAZI BAKERY

Visit an Eastern European bakery and you will find the shelves filled with a wide selection of delectable pastries, sweetmeats, crisp cookies, cakes and crunchy rolls. No one could possibly walk through without having a "little something". A cup of coffee is never just a cup of coffee: you must have a Danish – a pastry filled with jam and topped with icing (frosting) – or a rugelach, or maybe a mohn cake or strudel, or perhaps an apfelkuchen. The choice and variety is seemingly endless.

Cakes of all kinds are baked in the Ashkenazi kitchen. Kuchen is closer to a sweet fruit bread than a cake. It is made from a moderately sweet dough, filled with fresh or dried fruit. Honey cake, also known as lekach, is

eaten for Rosh Hashanah and Shabbat, while almond cakes, plava and other leaven-free cakes are classic Pesach specialities. For Purim, the traditional treat is hamantashen, triangular cakes filled with seeds and fruit that resemble the three-cornered hat of Haman.

Cookies and sweet biscuits include croissant-shaped rugelach, almond mandelbrot and plain kichel. None of these are very sweet, and they make the perfect accompaniment to tea or coffee. Teiglach, from Lithuania, are rich with honey, so a little goes a very long way.

Candied orange peel known as pomerantzen is a great favourite of all Jews, not just because it tastes so good, but because the peel that might otherwise have been discarded is transformed into an irresistible treat.

Jews love pastries, the most well known being strudel, which originated as a hefty pastry roll filled with

Left: Pomerantzen (candied citrus peel) is a classic Ashkenazi sweetmeat.

Below: Sweet, fruit-filled strudel made with paper-thin pastry is one of the glories of the Eastern European Jews.

vegetables or fruit. It was the Turks, invading Hungary in 1526, who introduced the thin multi-layered pastry that we now know as strudel dough.

Strudel is eaten for many festivals: with cabbage for Simchat Torah; with dried fruit for Tu b'Shevat; with crushed poppy-seed paste for Purim and with cheese for Shavuot. Fruit versions are filled with sliced apple, cherries or rhubarb, alone or with dried fruit.

Left: Traditional Ashkenazi rugelach and mandelbrot cookies are delicious with a glass of hot tea.

Making Strudel Pastry

This is very like filo pastry, which can be bought ready-made and makes a good substitute for strudel pastry.

1 In a large bowl, beat 250g/9oz/ generous 1 cup butter with 30ml/2 tbsp sugar and 250ml/8fl oz/1 cup sour cream or softened vanilla ice cream. Add 2.5ml/½ tsp vanilla or almond essence (extract) and 1.5ml/¼ tsp salt, then stir in 500g/1¼lb/5 cups plain (all-purpose) flour. Mix to a soft dough.

2 Divide the dough into three pieces, wrap separately and chill overnight. (It may be frozen for up to 3 months.)

3 If necessary, thaw the dough. Place one piece on a floured board. Flatten it lightly, then, very gently, pull it out with your hands, pulling each side in turn until it is almost paper thin. It is now ready to fill and bake. (Take extra care if you have long fingernails.)

VARIATION

To make a non-dairy pastry, substitute 120ml/4fl oz/½ cup each of sweet wine and vegetable oil for the butter and sour cream or ice cream.

SEPHARDI SWEET SPECIALITIES

These are Mediterranean in their origin. Every Sephardi community produces a wealth of moist, succulent almond and walnut cakes. Often a local dish was adapted for Jewish holidays – Greek Jews eat crisp, fried loukomades for Chanukkah, Israelis eat jam-filled sufganiot (doughnuts) and Tunisians enjoy syrup-soaked cakes for Purim.

During Pesach when leaven (and flour) may not be used, nuts are used to give body to desserts. Almond cakes and coconut macaroons are particularly popular, as is sesame seed halva.

Syrup-soaked filo pastries, such as nut-filled baklava, are popular among Sephardi Jews. Other pastries include kaddaif, a shredded pastry drenched in syrup, and felabis, deep-fried, pretzel-like pastries filled with syrup.

Making Simple Baklava

The secret to perfect baklava is to pour very cold syrup over a hot pastry, or very hot syrup over a cold pastry.

1 Preheat the oven to 200°C/400°F/ Gas 6. Layer six sheets of filo pastry in a shallow dish, brushing each layer with melted butter or oil.

2 Sprinkle chopped nuts on top of the pastry, to a depth of 1cm/½in. Sprinkle generously with sugar and cinnamon. Top with six more layers of buttered or oiled filo, then, using a sharp knife, cut the top layer of pastry into triangles.

3 Bake the baklava for 30 minutes until golden. Remove from the oven and pour over hattar, or a light syrup flavoured with orange flower water or rose water.

The Deli Cheesecake

This is one of the most popular desserts in the deli cabinet. It is often associated with Ashkenazim from Germany, who were famous for their fresh cheeses. It is eaten at Shavuot, reflecting the legend of the Jews who, on returning to camp after receiving the Torah, found that their milk had turned sour and had to sweeten it with honey.

Cheesecakes can be flavoured and topped with many ingredients from fruit to chocolate and it is not unusual to find delis offering upwards of 30 different types.

Below: Cheesecake is a deli classic, though purists argue that only a simple white cheesecake can be considered the real thing.

APPETIZERS
AND SOUPS

*Festive meals, from the weekly Shabbat to annual holidays,
almost always include a selection of appetizers. In fact, what
often distinguishes an everyday meal from a celebration is the
serving of these delicacies. Warming, stew-like soups, on the
other hand, have provided everyday sustenance in times of
scarcity and deprivation throughout Jewish history.*

BABA GHANOUSH

THE QUANTITIES IN THIS RICHLY FLAVOURED MIDDLE EASTERN AUBERGINE DIP CAN BE VARIED
ACCORDING TO TASTE. ADJUST THE AMOUNT OF AUBERGINE, GARLIC AND LEMON JUICE DEPENDING
ON HOW CREAMY, GARLICKY OR TART YOU WANT THE DIP TO BE.

2 Put the aubergine(s) in a plastic bag or in a bowl and seal tightly. Leave to cool for 30–60 minutes.

3 Peel off the blackened skin from the aubergine(s), reserving the juices. Chop the aubergine flesh, either by hand for a textured result or in a food processor for a smooth purée. Put the aubergine in a bowl and stir in the reserved juices.

4 Add the garlic and tahini to the aubergine and stir until smooth and well combined. Stir in the lemon juice, which will thicken the mixture. If the mixture becomes too thick, add 15–30ml/1–2 tbsp water or more lemon juice, if you like. Season with cumin and salt to taste.

SERVES TWO TO FOUR

INGREDIENTS
  1 large or 2 medium
    aubergines (eggplant)
  2–4 garlic cloves, chopped, to taste
  90–150ml/6–10 tbsp tahini
  juice of 1 lemon, or to taste
  1.5ml/¼ tsp ground cumin, or
    to taste
  salt
  extra virgin olive oil, for drizzling
  coriander (cilantro) leaves, hot
    pepper sauce and a few olives
    and/or pickled cucumbers and
    (bell) peppers, to garnish
  pitta bread or chunks of crusty
    French bread, to serve

1 Place the aubergine(s) directly over the flame of a gas stove or on the coals of a barbecue. Turn the aubergine(s) fairly frequently until deflated and the skin is evenly charred. Remove from the heat with a pair of tongs.

5 Spoon the mixture into a serving bowl. Drizzle with olive oil and garnish with fresh coriander leaves, hot pepper sauce and olives and/or pickled cucumbers and peppers. Serve at room temperature with pitta bread or chunks of crusty French bread.

HUMMUS

THIS CLASSIC MIDDLE EASTERN DISH IS MADE FROM COOKED CHICKPEAS, GROUND TO A PASTE AND FLAVOURED WITH GARLIC, LEMON JUICE, TAHINI, OLIVE OIL AND CUMIN. IT IS DELICIOUS SERVED WITH WEDGES OF TOASTED PITTA BREAD OR CRUDITÉS.

SERVES FOUR TO SIX

INGREDIENTS
  400g/14oz can chickpeas, drained
  60ml/4 tbsp tahini
  2–3 garlic cloves, chopped
  juice of ½–1 lemon
  cayenne pepper
  small pinch to 1.5ml/¼ tsp ground
    cumin, or more to taste
  salt and ground black pepper

VARIATION
Process 2 roasted red (bell) peppers with the chickpeas, then continue as above. Serve sprinkled with lightly toasted pine nuts and paprika mixed with olive oil.

1 Using a potato masher or food processor, coarsely mash the chickpeas. If you prefer a smoother purée, process them in a food processor or blender until smooth.

2 Mix the tahini into the chickpeas, then stir in the garlic, lemon juice, cayenne, cumin and salt and pepper to taste. If needed, add a little water. Serve at room temperature.

BULGARIAN CUCUMBER <u>AND</u> WALNUT APPETIZER

MANY BULGARIAN JEWS CAME TO ISRAEL BRINGING WITH THEM THEIR PASSION FOR EXCELLENT YOGURTS, WHICH ARE OFTEN USED IN SALADS. WHEN MADE WITH VERY THICK GREEK YOGURT, THIS APPETIZER CAN BE SHAPED INTO BALLS AND SERVED ON SALAD LEAVES.

SERVES SIX

INGREDIENTS

1 large cucumber
3–5 garlic cloves, finely chopped
250ml/8fl oz/1 cup sour cream or
  120ml/4fl oz/½ cup Greek
  (US strained plain) yogurt mixed
  with 120ml/4fl oz/½ cup double
  (heavy) cream
250ml/8fl oz/1 cup yogurt, preferably
  thick Greek or Bulgarian sheep's
  milk yogurt
2–3 large pinches of dried dill or
  30–45ml/2–3 tbsp chopped
  fresh dill
45–60ml/3–4 tbsp chopped walnuts
salt
sprig of dill, to garnish (optional)

1 Do not peel the cucumber. Using a sharp knife, dice it finely and place in a large mixing bowl.

2 Add the garlic, sour cream or yogurt and cream, yogurt, dill and salt. Mix together, then cover and chill.

3 To serve, pile the mixture into a bowl and sprinkle with walnuts. Garnish with dill, if you like.

MINT <u>AND</u> PARSLEY TAHINI SALAD

TAHINI IS A CREAMY SESAME SEED PASTE THAT IS WIDELY USED IN ISRAELI AND ARAB COOKING. ITS ALMOST DRY FLAVOUR COMBINES WONDERFULLY WITH FRESH HERBS AND SUBTLE SPICES IN THIS SALAD TO MAKE A LIGHT AND REFRESHING APPETIZER.

SERVES FOUR TO SIX

INGREDIENTS

115g/4oz/½ cup tahini
3 garlic cloves, chopped
½ bunch (about 20g/¾oz) fresh
  mint, chopped
½ bunch (about 20g/¾oz) fresh
  coriander (cilantro), chopped
½ bunch (about 20g/¾oz) fresh flat
  leaf parsley, chopped
juice of ½ lemon, or to taste
pinch of ground cumin
pinch of ground turmeric
pinch of ground cardamom seeds
cayenne pepper, to taste
salt
extra virgin olive oil, warmed pitta
  bread, olives and raw vegetables,
  to serve

1 Combine the tahini with the chopped garlic, fresh herbs and lemon juice in a bowl. Taste and add a little more lemon juice, if you like. Stir in a little water if the mixture seems too dense and thick. Alternatively, place the ingredients in a food processor. Process briefly, then stir in a little water if required.

2 Stir in the cumin, turmeric and cardamom to taste, then season with salt and cayenne pepper.

3 To serve, spoon into a shallow bowl or on to plates and drizzle with olive oil. Serve with warmed pitta bread, olives and raw vegetables.

MATZO BREI

EVERY ASHKENAZI FAMILY HAS ITS OWN VERSION OF THIS DISH OF SOAKED MATZOS, MIXED WITH EGG AND FRIED UNTIL CRISP. SOME RECIPES USE WATER, SOME MILK, OTHERS USE LOTS OF EGG, A VERY LITTLE EGG, OR EVEN NONE AT ALL. THIS VERSION IS CRISP, SALTY AND BROKEN INTO PIECES.

SERVES ONE

INGREDIENTS
3 matzos, broken into bitesize pieces
2 eggs, lightly beaten
30–45ml/2–3 tbsp olive oil or
  25–40g/1–1½oz/2–3 tbsp butter
salt
sour cream and fresh dill,
  to serve (optional)

VARIATION
To make a sweet matzo brei pancake, soak the matzos in 250ml/8fl oz/1 cup milk for 5–10 minutes. Add the eggs, a large pinch of ground cinnamon, 15–30ml/ 1–2 tbsp sugar and 2.5ml/½ tsp vanilla essence (extract). Fry the mixture in the oil or butter, turning once. Serve with jam or cinnamon sugar and sour cream.

1 Put the matzos in a large bowl and pour over cold water to cover. Leave for 2–3 minutes, then drain. Add the eggs.

2 Heat the oil or butter in a frying pan, then add the matzo mixture. Lower the heat and cook for 2–3 minutes until the bottom is golden brown.

3 Break up the matzo brei into pieces, turn them over and brown their other side. Turn once or twice again until the pieces are crisp. (The more times you turn them, the smaller the pieces will become.) Sprinkle with a little salt and serve immediately, with sour cream and dill if you like.

SMOKY AUBERGINE AND PEPPER SALAD

COOKING THE AUBERGINES WHOLE, OVER AN OPEN FLAME, GIVES THEM A DISTINCTIVE SMOKY FLAVOUR AND AROMA, AS WELL AS TENDER, CREAMY FLESH. THE SUBTLE FLAVOUR OF THE ROASTED AUBERGINE CONTRASTS WONDERFULLY WITH THE STRONG, SWEET FLAVOUR OF THE PEPPERS.

SERVES FOUR TO SIX

INGREDIENTS

2 aubergines (eggplant)
2 red (bell) peppers
3–5 garlic cloves, chopped, or more
  to taste
2.5ml/$\frac{1}{2}$ tsp ground cumin
juice of $\frac{1}{2}$–1 lemon, to taste
2.5ml/$\frac{1}{2}$ tsp sherry or wine vinegar
45–60ml/3–4 tbsp extra virgin
  olive oil
1–2 shakes of cayenne pepper,
  Tabasco or other hot pepper sauce
coarse sea salt
chopped fresh coriander (cilantro),
  to garnish
pitta bread wedges or thinly sliced
  French bread or ciabatta bread,
  sesame seed crackers and cucumber
  slices, to serve

1 Place the aubergines and peppers directly over a medium-low gas flame or on the coals of a barbecue. Turn the vegetables frequently until deflated and the skins are evenly charred.

2 Put the aubergines and peppers in a plastic bag or in a bowl and seal tightly. Leave to cool for 30–40 minutes.

3 Peel the vegetables, reserving the juices, and roughly chop the flesh. Put the flesh in a bowl and add the juices, garlic, cumin, lemon juice, vinegar, olive oil, hot pepper seasoning and salt. Mix well to combine. Turn the mixture into a serving bowl and garnish with coriander. Serve with bread, sesame seed crackers and cucumber slices.

OLD COUNTRY MUSHROOM, BEAN AND BARLEY SOUP

THIS HEARTY ASHKENAZI SOUP IS PERFECT ON A FREEZING COLD DAY. SERVE IN WARMED BOWLS, WITH PLENTY OF RYE OR PUMPERNICKEL BREAD.

SERVES SIX TO EIGHT

INGREDIENTS
30–45ml/2–3 tbsp small haricot
 (navy) beans, soaked overnight
45–60ml/ 3–4 tbsp green split peas
45–60ml/3–4 tbsp yellow split peas
90–105ml/6–7 tbsp pearl barley
1 onion, chopped
2 carrots, sliced
3 celery sticks, diced or sliced
½ baking potato, peeled and cut
 into chunks
10g/¼oz or 45ml/3 tbsp mixed
 flavourful dried mushrooms
5 garlic cloves, sliced
2 litres/3½ pints/8 cups water
2 vegetable stock (bouillon) cubes
salt and ground black pepper
30–45ml/2–3 tbsp chopped fresh
 parsley, to garnish

1 In a large pan, put the beans, green and yellow split peas, pearl barley, onion, carrots, celery, potato, mushrooms, garlic and water.

2 Bring the mixture to the boil, then reduce the heat, cover and simmer gently for about 1½ hours, or until the beans are tender.

3 Crumble the stock cubes into the soup and taste for seasoning. Ladle into warmed bowls, garnish with parsley and serve with rye or pumpernickel bread.

COOK'S TIP
Do not add the stock cubes until the end of cooking as the salt will prevent the beans from becoming tender.

SWEET AND SOUR CABBAGE, BEETROOT AND TOMATO BORSCHT

THERE ARE MANY VARIATIONS OF THIS CLASSIC ASHKENAZI SOUP, WHICH MAY BE SERVED HOT OR COLD. THIS VERSION INCLUDES PLENTIFUL AMOUNTS OF CABBAGE, TOMATOES AND POTATOES.

SERVES SIX

INGREDIENTS
1 onion, chopped
1 carrot, chopped
4–6 raw or vacuum-packed (cooked, not pickled) beetroot (beets), 3–4 diced and 1–2 coarsely grated
400g/14oz can tomatoes
4–6 new potatoes, cut into bitesize pieces
1 small white cabbage, thinly sliced
1 litre/1¾ pints/4 cups vegetable stock
45ml/3 tbsp sugar
30–45ml/2–3 tbsp white wine, cider vinegar or sour salt (citric acid)
45ml/3 tbsp chopped fresh dill, plus extra to garnish
salt and ground black pepper
sour cream, to garnish
buttered rye bread, to serve

1 Put the onion, carrot, diced beetroot, tomatoes, potatoes, cabbage and stock in a large pan. Bring to the boil, reduce the heat and simmer for 30 minutes, or until the potatoes are tender.

VARIATIONS
To make meat borscht, place 1kg/2¼lb chopped beef in a large pan. Pour over water to cover and crumble in 1 beef stock (bouillon) cube. Bring to the boil, then reduce the heat and simmer until tender. Skim any fat from the surface, then add the vegetables and proceed as above. For Kashrut, omit the sour cream and serve with unbuttered rye bread.

2 Add the grated beetroot, sugar and wine, vinegar or sour salt to the soup and cook for 10 minutes. Taste for a good sweet-sour balance and add more sugar and/or vinegar if necessary. Season.

3 Stir the chopped dill into the soup and ladle into warmed bowls immediately. Garnish each bowl with a generous spoonful of sour cream and more dill and serve with buttered rye bread.

FRAGRANT BEETROOT AND VEGETABLE SOUP WITH SPICED LAMB KUBBEH

THE JEWISH COMMUNITY FROM COCHIN IN INDIA IS SCATTERED NOW BUT THEY ARE STILL FAMOUS FOR THEIR CUISINE. THIS TANGY SOUP IS SERVED WITH DUMPLINGS MADE OF BRIGHT YELLOW PASTA WRAPPED AROUND A SPICY LAMB FILLING AND A DOLLOP OF FRAGRANT GREEN HERB PASTE.

SERVES SIX TO EIGHT

INGREDIENTS
15ml/1 tbsp vegetable oil
½ onion, finely chopped
6 garlic cloves
1 carrot, diced
1 courgette (zucchini), diced
½ celery stick, diced (optional)
4–5 cardamom pods
2.5ml/½ tsp curry powder
4 vacuum-packed beetroot (beets)
   (cooked not pickled), finely diced
   and juice reserved
1 litre/1¾ pints/4 cups
   vegetable stock
400g/14oz can chopped tomatoes
45–60ml/3–4 tbsp chopped fresh
   coriander (cilantro) leaves
2 bay leaves
15ml/1 tbsp sugar
salt and ground black pepper
15–30ml/1–2 tbsp white wine
   vinegar, to serve
For the kubbeh
2 large pinches of saffron threads
15ml/1 tbsp hot water
15ml/1 tbsp vegetable oil
1 large onion, chopped
250g/9oz lean minced (ground) lamb
5ml/1 tsp vinegar
½ bunch fresh mint, chopped
115g/4oz/1 cup plain (all-purpose) flour
2–3 pinches of salt
2.5–5ml/½–1 tsp ground turmeric
45–60ml/3–4 tbsp cold water
For the ginger and coriander paste
4 garlic cloves, chopped
15–25ml/1–1½ tbsp chopped
   fresh root ginger
½–4 fresh mild chillies
½ large bunch fresh coriander
   (cilantro)
30ml/2 tbsp white wine vinegar
extra virgin olive oil

COOK'S TIP
Serve any leftover paste with meatballs or spread on sandwiches.

1 To make the paste, put the garlic, ginger and chillies in a food processor and process. Add the coriander, vinegar, oil and salt and process to a purée. Set aside.

2 To make the kubbeh filling, place the saffron and hot water in a small bowl and leave to infuse (steep). Meanwhile, heat the oil in a pan and fry the onion until softened. Put the onion and saffron water in a food processor and blend. Add the lamb, season and blend. Add the vinegar and mint, then chill.

3 To make the kubbeh dough, put the flour, salt and ground turmeric in a food processor, then gradually add the water, processing until it forms a sticky dough. Knead on a floured surface for 5 minutes, wrap in a plastic bag and leave to stand for 30 minutes.

4 Divide the dough into 10–15 pieces. Roll each into a ball, then, using a pasta machine, roll into very thin rounds.

5 Lay the rounds on a well-floured surface. Place a spoonful of filling in the middle of each. Dampen the edges of the dough, then bring them together and seal. Set aside on a floured surface.

6 To make the soup, heat the oil in a pan, add the onion and fry for about 10 minutes, or until softened but not browned. Add half the garlic, the carrot, courgette, celery, if using, cardamom pods and curry powder, and cook for 2–3 minutes.

7 Add three of the diced beetroot, the stock, tomatoes, coriander, bay leaves and sugar to the pan. Bring to the boil, then reduce the heat and simmer for about 20 minutes.

8 Add the remaining beetroot, beetroot juice and garlic to the soup. Season with salt and pepper to taste and set aside until ready to serve.

9 To serve, reheat the soup and poach the dumplings in a large pan of salted boiling water for about 4 minutes. Using a slotted spoon, remove the dumplings from the water as they are cooked and place on a plate to keep warm.

10 Ladle the soup into bowls, adding a dash of vinegar to each bowl, then add two or three dumplings and a small spoonful of the ginger and coriander paste to each. Serve immediately.

MEAT AND POULTRY

For the Jews of the shtetl, high prices — reflecting the trained skills of the shochet and the taxes that were made on kosher meat — meant that eating meat tended to be little more than having a few shreds of brisket cooked with potatoes. In contrast, classic Ashkenazi dishes include braised and minced (ground) meats, rich with the robust flavours of onions and herbs. Jewish meat dishes can also be aromatic, flavoured with the Eastern spices of the Sephardi kitchen — particularly the grilled meats from Israel and the Middle East.

SWEET AND SOUR TONGUE

Tongue is a favourite meat in the Ashkenazi kitchen, although in recent years it has rather gone out of fashion. It is wonderful served hot with a sweet-and-sour sauce and leftovers are good cold, without the sauce, thinly sliced for sandwiches or a salad.

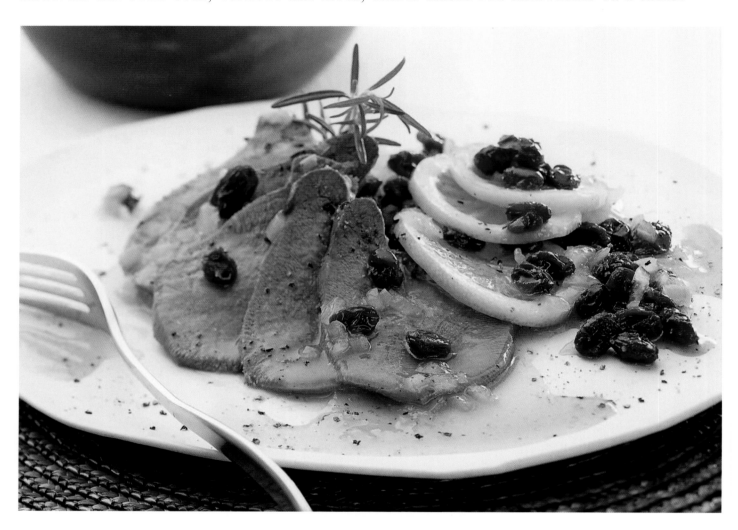

SERVES ABOUT EIGHT

INGREDIENTS

1kg/2¼lb fresh ox tongue
2–3 onions, 1 sliced and
  1–2 chopped
3 bay leaves
½–1 stock (bouillon) cube or a
  small amount of stock powder
  or bouillon
45ml/3 tbsp vegetable oil
60ml/4 tbsp potato flour
120ml/4fl oz/½ cup honey
150g/5oz/1 cup raisins
2.5ml/½ tsp salt
2.5ml/½ tsp ground ginger
1 lemon, sliced
fresh rosemary sprigs, to garnish

1 Put the tongue, sliced onion and bay leaves in a large pan. Pour over cold water to cover and add the stock cube, powder or bouillon. Bring to the boil, reduce the heat, cover and simmer gently for 2–3 hours. Leave to cool.

2 In a small frying pan, heat the oil, add the chopped onion and cook for about 5 minutes, until softened.

3 Stir the potato flour into the onions and gradually add about 500ml/17fl oz/ 2¼ cups of the stock, stirring constantly to prevent lumps forming.

4 Stir the honey, raisins, salt and ginger into the sauce and continue to cook until it has thickened and is smooth. Add the lemon slices and set the sauce aside.

5 Slice the tongue thinly and serve generously coated with the sweet-and-sour sauce. Garnish with rosemary.

POT-ROASTED BRISKET

THIS BIG, POT-ROASTED MEAT DISH INCLUDES THE TRADITIONAL KISHKE, A HEAVY, SAUSAGE-SHAPED DUMPLING, WHICH IS ADDED TO THE POT AND COOKED WITH THE MEAT. SERVE WITH KASHA VARNISHKES — MEAT GRAVY WITH KASHA IS ONE OF LIFE'S PERFECT COMBINATIONS.

SERVES SIX TO EIGHT

INGREDIENTS
    5 onions, sliced
    3 bay leaves
    1–1.6kg/2¼–3½lb beef brisket
    1 garlic head, broken into cloves
    4 carrots, thickly sliced
    5–10ml/1–2 tsp paprika
    about 500ml/17fl oz/2¼ cups
        beef stock
    3–4 baking potatoes, peeled
        and quartered
    salt and ground black pepper
For the kishke
    about 90cm/36in sausage casing
        (see Cook's Tip)
    250g/9oz/2¼ cups plain
        (all-purpose) flour
    120ml/4fl oz/½ cup semolina
        or couscous
    10–15ml/2–3 tsp paprika
    1 carrot, grated and 2 carrots,
        diced (optional)
    250ml/8fl oz/1 cup rendered
        chicken fat
    30ml/2 tbsp crisp, fried onions
    ½ onion, grated and 3 onions,
        thinly sliced
    3 garlic cloves, chopped
    salt and ground black pepper

2 Pour in enough stock to fill the dish to about 5–7.5cm/2–3in and cover with foil. Cook in the oven for 2 hours.

3 Meanwhile, make the kishke. In a bowl, combine all the ingredients and stuff the mixture into the casing, leaving enough space for the mixture to expand. Tie into sausage-shaped lengths.

4 When the meat has cooked for about 2 hours, add the kishke and potatoes to the pan, re-cover and cook for a further 1 hour, or until the meat and potatoes are tender.

5 Remove the foil from the dish and increase the oven temperature to 190–200°C/375–400°F/Gas 5–6. Move the onions away from the top of the meat to the side of the dish and return to the oven for a further 30 minutes, or until the meat, onions and potatoes are beginning to brown and become crisp. Serve hot or cold.

COOK'S TIP
Traditionally, sausage casings are used for kishke but, if unavailable, use cooking-strength clear film (plastic wrap) or a piece of muslin (cheesecloth).

1 Preheat the oven to 180°C/350°F/ Gas 4. Put one-third of the onions and a bay leaf in an ovenproof dish, then top with the brisket. Sprinkle over the garlic, carrots and the remaining bay leaves, sprinkle with salt, pepper and paprika, then top with the remaining onions.

KOFTA KEBABS

THESE SPICY PATTIES OF MINCED LAMB ARE SPIKED WITH AROMATIC HERBS AND SEASONINGS. THEY ARE VERY POPULAR IN BOTH JEWISH COMMUNITIES AND NON-JEWISH COMMUNITIES FROM THE MIDDLE EAST THROUGH TO THE INDIAN SUBCONTINENT. SERVE WITH FLATBREAD AND A SELECTION OF SALADS, SUCH AS ORANGES SPRINKLED WITH CAYENNE OR PAPRIKA, ONIONS SPRINKLED WITH SUMAC, AND TOMATO WEDGES WITH HERBS AND CHILLIES.

SERVES FOUR

INGREDIENTS
    450g/1lb minced (ground) lamb
    1–2 large slices of French bread,
      very finely crumbled
    ½ bunch fresh coriander (cilantro),
      finely chopped
    5 garlic cloves, chopped
    1 onion, finely chopped
    juice of ½ lemon
    5ml/1 tsp ground cumin
    5ml/1 tsp paprika
    15ml/1 tbsp curry powder
    pinch each of ground cardamom,
      turmeric and cinnamon
    15ml/1 tbsp tomato purée (paste)
    cayenne pepper or chopped fresh
      chillies (optional)
    1 egg, beaten, if needed
    salt and ground black pepper
    flat bread and salads, to serve

1 Put the lamb, crumbled bread, coriander, garlic, onion, lemon juice, spices, tomato purée, cayenne pepper or chillies and seasoning in a large bowl. Mix well. If the mixture does not bind together, add the beaten egg and a little more bread.

2 With wet hands, shape the mixture into four large or eight small patties.

3 Heat a heavy non-stick frying pan, add the patties and cook, taking care that they do not fall apart, turning once or twice, until browned. Serve hot with flat bread and salads.

VARIATION
Mix a handful of raisins or sultanas (golden raisins) into the meat mixture before shaping it into patties.

JERUSALEM BARBECUED LAMB KEBABS

IN THE EARLY DAYS OF THE MODERN STATE OF ISRAEL, THE DAYS OF AUSTERITY, "LAMB" KEBABS WOULD HAVE BEEN MADE WITH TURKEY AND A LITTLE LAMB FAT, AND "VEAL" KEBABS WITH CHICKEN AND A SMALL AMOUNT OF VEAL. TURKEY, CHICKEN, BEEF AND VEAL CAN ALL BE COOKED IN THIS WAY.

SERVES FOUR TO SIX

INGREDIENTS

800g/1¾lb tender lamb, cubed
1.5ml/¼ tsp ground allspice
1.5ml/¼ tsp ground cinnamon
1.5ml/¼ tsp ground black pepper
1.5ml/¼ tsp ground cardamom
45–60ml/3–4 tbsp chopped
  fresh parsley
2 onions, chopped
5–8 garlic cloves, chopped
juice of ½ lemon or 45ml/3 tbsp dry
  white wine
45ml/3 tbsp extra virgin olive oil
sumac, for sprinkling (optional)
30ml/2 tbsp pine nuts
salt
For serving
  flat breads, such as pitta bread,
    tortillas or naan bread
  tahini
  crunchy vegetable salad

3 Thread the cubes of meat on to wooden or metal skewers, then cook on the barbecue for 2–3 minutes on each side, turning occasionally, until cooked evenly and browned.

4 Transfer the kebabs to a serving dish and sprinkle with the reserved onions, parsley, sumac, if using, pine nuts and salt, if you like. Serve the kebabs with warmed flat breads to wrap the kebabs in, a bowl of tahini for drizzling over and a vegetable salad.

COOK'S TIPS
• If sumac is available, its tangy flavour is fresh and invigorating, and its red colour is appealing.
• These kebabs can also be cooked under a hot grill (broiler).

1 Put the lamb, allspice, cinnamon, black pepper, cardamom, half the parsley, half the onions, the garlic, lemon juice or wine and olive oil in a bowl and mix together. Season with salt now, if you prefer, or sprinkle on after cooking. Set aside and leave to marinate.

2 Meanwhile, light the barbecue and leave for about 40 minutes. When the coals are white and grey, the barbecue is ready for cooking. If using wooden skewers, soak them in water for about 30 minutes to prevent them from burning.

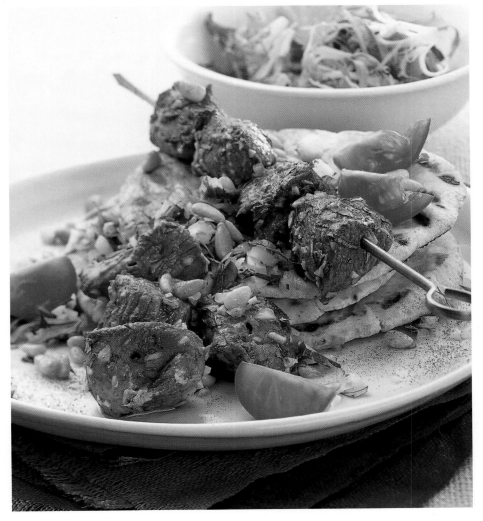

LAMB POT-ROASTED WITH TOMATOES, BEANS AND ONIONS

THIS SLOW-BRAISED DISH OF LAMB AND TOMATOES, SPICED WITH CINNAMON AND STEWED WITH GREEN BEANS, SHOWS A GREEK INFLUENCE. IT IS ALSO GOOD MADE WITH COURGETTES INSTEAD OF BEANS.

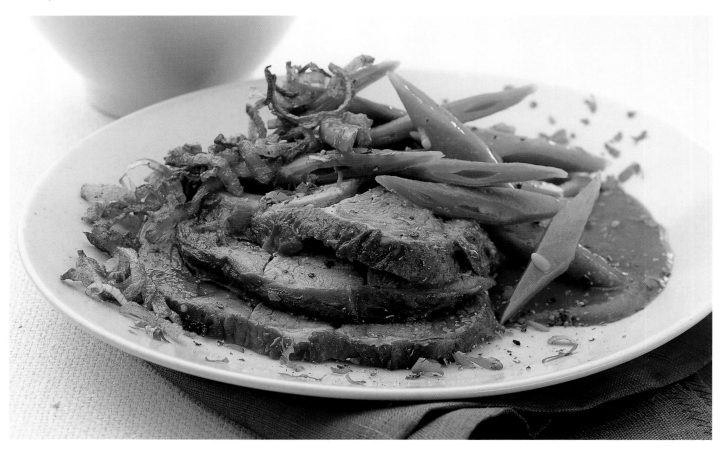

SERVES EIGHT

INGREDIENTS

1kg/2¼lb lamb on the bone
8 garlic cloves, chopped
2.5–5ml/½–1 tsp ground cumin
45ml/3 tbsp olive oil
juice of 1 lemon
2 onions, thinly sliced
about 500ml/17fl oz/2¼ cups
  lamb, beef or vegetable stock
75–90ml/5–6 tbsp tomato
  purée (paste)
1 cinnamon stick
2–3 large pinches of ground
  allspice or ground cloves
15–30ml/1–2 tbsp sugar
400g/14oz/scant 3 cups runner
  (green) beans
salt and ground black pepper
15–30ml/1–2 tbsp chopped
  fresh parsley, to garnish

1 Preheat the oven to 160°C/325°F/Gas 3. Coat the lamb with the garlic, cumin, olive oil, lemon juice, salt and pepper.

2 Heat a flameproof casserole. Sear the lamb on all sides. Add the onions and pour the stock over the meat to cover. Stir in the tomato purée, spices and sugar. Cover and cook in the oven for 2–3 hours.

3 Remove the casserole from the oven and pour the stock into a pan. Move the onions to the side of the dish and return to the oven, uncovered, for 20 minutes.

4 Meanwhile, add the beans to the hot stock and cook until the beans are tender and the sauce has thickened. Slice the meat and serve with the pan juices and beans. Garnish with parsley.

ISRAELI BARBECUED CHICKEN

BARBECUED CHICKEN IS UBIQUITOUS TO ISRAEL AND IT SEEMS THAT EVERY STREET CORNER KIOSK AND STALL SELLS A VERSION OF THIS AROMATIC TREAT. IN THIS RECIPE, THE EGYPTIAN-INSPIRED MARINADE IS STRONGLY SCENTED WITH CUMIN AND CINNAMON.

SERVES FOUR

INGREDIENTS
    5 garlic cloves, chopped
    30ml/2 tbsp ground cumin
    7.5ml/1½ tsp ground cinnamon
    5ml/1 tsp paprika
    juice of 1 lemon
    30ml/2 tbsp olive oil
    1.3kg/3lb chicken, cut into
      8 portions
    salt and ground black pepper
    fresh coriander (cilantro) leaves,
      to garnish
    warmed pitta bread, salad and
      lemon wedges, to serve

VARIATION
For a Yemenite flavour, use 7.5ml/
1½ tsp turmeric and a pinch of ground
cardamom in place of the cinnamon.

1 In a bowl, combine the garlic, cumin, cinnamon, paprika, lemon juice, oil, salt and pepper. Add the chicken and turn to coat thoroughly. Leave to marinate for at least 1 hour or cover and place in the refrigerator overnight.

2 Light the barbecue. After about 40 minutes it will be ready for cooking.

3 Arrange the dark meat on the grill and cook for 10 minutes, turning once.

4 Place the remaining chicken on the grill and cook for 7–10 minutes, turning occasionally, until golden brown and the juices run clear when pricked with a skewer. Serve immediately, with pitta breads, lemon wedges and salad.

CHICKEN, SPLIT PEA AND AUBERGINE KORESH

THIS IS A CALIFORNIAN VERSION OF THE TRADITIONAL PERSIAN KORESH, A THICK, SAUCY STEW SERVED WITH RICE, WHICH IS A MAINSTAY OF THE PERSIAN TABLE. IN IRAN, LAMB WAS OFTEN THE MEAT OF CHOICE BUT IN SUNNY CALIFORNIA THIS HEARTY MEAT DISH HAS BEEN TRANSFORMED TO A LIGHT CHICKEN, TOMATO AND SPLIT PEA STEW.

SERVES FOUR TO SIX

INGREDIENTS

  50g/2oz/¼ cup green split peas
  45–60ml/3–4 tbsp olive oil
  1 large or 2 small onions,
    finely chopped
  500g/1¼lb boneless
    chicken thighs
  500ml/17fl oz/2¼ cups
    chicken stock
  5ml/1 tsp ground turmeric
  2.5ml/½ tsp ground cinnamon
  1.5ml/¼ tsp grated nutmeg
  2 aubergines (eggplant), diced
  8–10 ripe tomatoes, diced
  2 garlic cloves, crushed
  30ml/2 tbsp dried mint
  salt and ground black pepper
  fresh mint, to garnish
  rice, to serve

1 Put the split peas in a bowl, pour over cold water to cover, then leave to soak for about 4 hours. Drain well.

2 Heat a little of the oil in a pan, add two-thirds of the onions and cook for about 5 minutes. Add the chicken and cook until golden brown on all sides.

3 Add the soaked split peas to the chicken mixture, then the stock, turmeric, cinnamon and nutmeg. Cook over a medium-low heat for about 40 minutes, until the split peas are tender.

VARIATION
To make a traditional lamb koresh, use 675g/1½lb lamb stew chunks in place of the chicken. Add to the onions, pour over water to cover and cook for 1½ hours until tender, then proceed as above.

4 Heat the remaining oil in a pan, add the aubergines and remaining onions and cook until lightly browned. Add the tomatoes, garlic and mint. Season.

5 Just before serving, stir the aubergine mixture into the chicken and split pea stew. Garnish with fresh mint leaves and serve with rice.

MILD GREEN CALCUTTA CURRY OF CHICKEN AND VEGETABLES

THE ADDITION OF COCONUT MILK CREATES A RICH SAUCE THAT IS SWEET WITH DRIED AND FRESH FRUIT AND FRAGRANT WITH HERBS. IT IS PERFECT FOR THOSE KEEPING KASHRUT AS IT HAS A CREAMY CHARACTER YET CONTAINS NO DAIRY PRODUCTS. SERVE WITH HOT NAAN OR STEAMED RICE.

SERVES FOUR

INGREDIENTS

   4 garlic cloves, chopped
   15ml/1 tbsp chopped fresh
     root ginger
   2–3 chillies, chopped
   ½ bunch fresh coriander (cilantro)
     leaves, roughly chopped
   1 onion, chopped
   juice of 1 lemon
   pinch of cayenne pepper
   2.5ml/½ tsp curry powder
   2.5ml/½ tsp ground cumin
   2–3 pinches of ground cloves
   large pinch of ground coriander
   3 boneless chicken breast portions
     or thighs, skinned and cut into
     bitesize pieces
   30ml/2 tbsp vegetable oil
   2 cinnamon sticks
   250ml/8fl oz/1 cup chicken stock
   250ml/8fl oz/1 cup coconut milk
   15–30ml/1–2 tbsp sugar
   1–2 bananas
   ¼ pineapple, peeled and chopped
   handful of sultanas (golden raisins)
   handful of raisins or currants
   2–3 sprigs of fresh mint, thinly sliced
   juice of ¼–½ lemon
   salt

1 Purée the garlic, ginger, chillies, fresh coriander, onion, lemon juice, cayenne pepper, curry powder, cumin, cloves, ground coriander and salt in a food processor or blender.

2 Toss together the chicken pieces with about 15–30ml/1–2 tbsp of the spice mixture and set aside.

3 Heat the oil in a wok or frying pan, then add the remaining spice mixture and cook over a medium heat, stirring, for 10 minutes, or until the paste is lightly browned.

4 Stir the cinnamon sticks, stock, coconut milk and sugar into the pan, bring to the boil, then reduce the heat and simmer for 10 minutes.

5 Stir the chicken into the sauce and cook for 2 minutes, or until the chicken becomes opaque.

6 Meanwhile, thickly slice the bananas. Stir all the fruit into the curry and cook for 1–2 minutes. Stir in the mint and lemon juice. Check the seasoning and add more salt, spice and lemon juice if necessary. Serve immediately.

FISH

Fish is pareve and so may be eaten with either meat or dairy foods. This provides great variety and flexibility within the otherwise demanding laws of Kashrut. Having fish as a main course means that you can serve an elegant entertaining menu that has butter, cheeses and rich dairy desserts, without worrying about the lack of meat. Both Ashkenazim and Sephardim have many traditional fish dishes, from the fried fish of London's East End to whole fish wrapped in pastry in Israel.

SCRAMBLED EGGS WITH LOX AND ONIONS

SERVE THIS QUINTESSENTIAL NEW YORK SUNDAY BRUNCH WITH PILES OF FRESHLY TOASTED BAGELS, MUGS OF COFFEE AND A SELECTION OF SUNDAY NEWSPAPERS.

SERVES FOUR

INGREDIENTS

40g/1½oz/3 tbsp unsalted
  (sweet) butter
2 onions, chopped
150–200g/5–7oz smoked
  salmon trimmings
6–8 eggs, lightly beaten
ground black pepper
45ml/3 tbsp chopped fresh chives,
  plus whole chives, to garnish
bagels, to serve

VARIATIONS
Substitute 200–250g/7–9oz diced
kosher salami for the smoked salmon
and cook in oil or pareve margerine.

1 Heat half the unsalted butter in a
frying pan, add the chopped onions
and fry until softened and just
beginning to brown. Add the smoked
salmon trimmings to the onions and
mix well to combine.

2 Pour the eggs into the pan and stir
until soft curds form. Add the remaining
butter and stir off the heat until creamy.
Season with pepper. Spoon on to
serving plates and garnish with chives.
Serve with bagels.

FILO-WRAPPED FISH

THIS DELICIOUS DISH COMES FROM JERUSALEM, WHERE WHOLE FISH ARE WRAPPED IN FILO PASTRY AND SERVED WITH A ZESTY TOMATO SAUCE. THE CHOICE OF FISH CAN BE VARIED ACCORDING TO WHAT IS IN SEASON AND WHAT IS FRESHEST ON THE DAY OF PURCHASE.

SERVES THREE TO FOUR

INGREDIENTS
　　450g/1lb salmon or cod steaks
　　　or fillets
　　1 lemon
　　30ml/2 tbsp olive oil, plus extra
　　　for brushing
　　1 onion, chopped
　　2 celery sticks, chopped
　　1 green (bell) pepper, diced
　　5 garlic cloves, chopped
　　400g/14oz fresh or canned
　　　tomatoes, chopped
　　120ml/4fl oz/½ cup passata
　　　(bottled strained tomatoes)
　　30ml/2 tbsp chopped fresh flat
　　　leaf parsley
　　2–3 pinches of ground allspice or
　　　ground cloves
　　cayenne pepper, to taste
　　pinch of sugar
　　about 130g/4½oz filo pastry
　　　(6–8 large sheets)
　　salt and ground black pepper

1 Sprinkle the salmon or cod steaks or fillets with salt and black pepper and a squeeze of lemon juice. Set aside while you prepare the sauce.

2 Heat the olive oil in a pan, add the chopped onion, celery and pepper and fry for about 5 minutes, until the vegetables are softened. Add the garlic and cook for a further 1 minute, then add the tomatoes and passata and cook until the tomatoes are of a sauce consistency.

3 Stir the parsley into the sauce, then season with allspice or cloves, cayenne pepper, sugar and salt and pepper.

4 Preheat the oven to 200°C/400°F/ Gas 6. Take a sheet of filo pastry, brush with a little olive oil and cover with a second sheet. Place a piece of fish on top of the pastry, towards the bottom edge, then top with 1–2 spoonfuls of the sauce, spreading it evenly.

5 Roll the fish in the pastry, taking care to enclose the filling completely. Arrange on a baking sheet and repeat with the remaining fish and pastry. You should have about half the sauce remaining, to serve with the fish.

6 Bake for 10–15 minutes, or until golden. Meanwhile, reheat the remaining sauce if necessary. Serve immediately with the remaining sauce.

MOROCCAN GRILLED FISH BROCHETTES

SERVE THESE DELICIOUS SKEWERS WITH POTATOES, AUBERGINE SLICES AND STRIPS OF RED PEPPERS, WHICH CAN BE COOKED ON THE BARBECUE ALONGSIDE THE FISH BROCHETTES. ACCOMPANY WITH A BOWL OF ZCHUG AND A STACK OF WARM, SOFT PITTA BREADS OR FLOUR TORTILLAS.

SERVES FOUR TO SIX

INGREDIENTS

    5 garlic cloves, chopped
    2.5ml/½ tsp paprika
    2.5ml/½ tsp ground cumin
    2.5–5ml/½–1 tsp salt
    2–3 pinches of cayenne pepper
    60ml/4 tbsp olive oil
    30ml/2 tbsp lemon juice
    30ml/2 tbsp chopped fresh coriander
    (cilantro) or parsley
    675g/1½lb firm-fleshed white fish,
    such as haddock, halibut, sea bass,
    snapper or turbot, cut into
    2.5–5cm/1–2in cubes
    3–4 green (bell) peppers, cut into
    2.5–5cm/1–2in pieces
    2 lemon wedges, to serve

1 Put the garlic, paprika, cumin, salt, cayenne pepper, oil, lemon juice and coriander or parsley in a large bowl and mix together. Add the fish and toss to coat. Leave to marinate for at least 30 minutes, and preferably 2 hours, at room temperature, or chill overnight.

2 About 40 minutes before you are going to cook the brochettes, light the barbecue. The barbecue is ready when the coals have turned white and grey.

3 Meanwhile, thread the fish cubes and pepper pieces alternately on to wooden or metal skewers.

4 Grill the brochettes on the barbecue for 2–3 minutes on each side, or until the fish is tender and lightly browned. Serve with lemon wedges.

COOK'S TIP
If you are using wooden skewers for the brochettes, soak them in cold water for 30 minutes before using to prevent them from burning.

YEMENITE POACHED FISH IN SPICY TOMATO HERB SAUCE

This traditional Jewish dish is known as Samak. Yemenite spicing is refreshing in the sultry heat of the Middle East and is very popular with Israelis. Serve this dish with flat breads such as pitta or matzos, and hilbeh, a tomato and fenugreek relish.

SERVES EIGHT

INGREDIENTS

300ml/½ pint/1¼ cups passata (bottled strained tomatoes)
150ml/¼ pint/⅔ cup fish stock
1 large onion, chopped
60ml/4 tbsp chopped fresh coriander (cilantro) leaves
60ml/4 tbsp chopped fresh parsley
5–8 garlic cloves, crushed
chopped fresh chilli or chilli paste, to taste
large pinch of ground ginger
large pinch of curry powder
1.5ml/¼ tsp ground cumin
1.5ml/¼ tsp ground turmeric
seeds from 2–3 cardamom pods
juice of 2 lemons, plus extra if needed
30ml/2 tbsp vegetable or olive oil
1.5kg/3¼lb mixed white fish fillets
salt and ground black pepper

1 Put the passata, stock, onion, herbs, garlic, chilli, ginger, curry powder, cumin, turmeric, cardamom, lemon juice and oil in a pan and bring to the boil.

VARIATIONS
• This dish is just as good using only one type of fish, such as cod or flounder.
• Instead of poaching the fish, wrap each piece in puff pastry and bake at 190°C/375°F/Gas 5 for 20 minutes, then serve with the tomato sauce.

2 Remove the pan from the heat and add the fish fillets to the hot sauce. Return to the heat and allow the sauce to boil briefly again. Reduce the heat and simmer very gently for about 5 minutes, or until the fish is tender. (Test the fish with a fork. If the flesh flakes easily, then it is cooked.)

3 Taste the sauce and adjust the seasoning, adding more lemon juice if necessary. Serve hot or warm.

BRITISH FRIED FISH PATTIES

THESE PATTIES ARE THE FRIED VERSION OF GEFILTE FISH AND ARE PROBABLY THE ORIGINAL WAY THAT THEY WERE MADE WHEN BROUGHT TO ENGLAND BY PORTUGUESE JEWS IN THE 16TH CENTURY.

2 The batter should be firm enough to shape into a soft patty. If it is too thin, add a little more matzo meal and if too thick, add 15–30ml/1–2 tbsp water. Cover and chill for at least 1 hour.

3 Form the mixture into round patties measuring about 6cm/2½in in diameter and 2cm/¾in thick.

4 Put some matzo meal on a plate and use to coat each patty. Place the coated patties on another plate.

5 Heat the oil in a pan until it is hot enough to brown a cube of bread in 30 seconds. Add the patties, taking care not to overcrowd the pan, and fry for 7–8 minutes, turning occasionally, until they are golden brown on both sides. Place on kitchen paper to drain. Serve hot or cold with one or more spicy condiments.

VARIATION

To make a Sephardi version, add a little chopped garlic to the fish mixture and fry the patties in olive oil.

MAKES TWELVE TO FOURTEEN

INGREDIENTS
    450g/1lb haddock fillet, skinned
    450g/1lb cod fillet, skinned
    2 eggs
    50–65g/2–2½oz matzo meal, plus
      extra for coating
    10ml/2 tsp salt
    5ml/1 tsp sugar
    15ml/1 tbsp vegetable oil
    15ml/1 tbsp chopped fresh parsley
    2 onions, chopped
    vegetable oil, for frying
    ground black pepper
    chrain or other spicy condiment,
      to serve

1 Mince (grind) or finely chop the fish in a food processor or by hand. Add the eggs, matzo meal, salt, sugar, oil, parsley, onions and a little pepper. Combine to form a batter.

GINGER FISHBALLS IN TOMATO AND PRESERVED LEMON SAUCE

THESE SPICY BALLS OF MINCED FISH AND GINGER, COOKED IN A SAUCE OF TOMATOES AND PRESERVED LEMON, ARE A SPECIALITY OF THE JEWS OF MOROCCO. ENJOY THEM ACCOMPANIED BY FLAT BREAD TO SCOOP UP THE DELICIOUS SAUCE AND LEMON, OR WITH COUSCOUS COOKED IN FISH STOCK.

SERVES SIX

INGREDIENTS

65g/2½oz bread (about 2 slices)
1kg/2¼lb minced (ground) fish such as cod, haddock or whiting
2 onions, chopped
8 garlic cloves, chopped
2.5–5ml/½–1 tsp ground turmeric
2.5ml/½ tsp ground ginger
2.5ml/½ tsp ras al hanout or garam masala
1 bunch fresh coriander (cilantro), chopped, plus extra to garnish
1 egg
cayenne pepper, to taste
150ml/¼ pint/⅔ cup vegetable or olive oil or a combination of both
4 ripe tomatoes, diced
5ml/1 tsp paprika
1 preserved lemon, rinsed and cut into small strips
salt and ground black pepper
½ lemon, cut into wedges, to serve

1 Remove the crusts from the bread, put the bread in a bowl and pour over cold water. Leave to soak for about 10 minutes, then squeeze dry.

2 Add the fish to the bread with half the onions, half the garlic, half the turmeric, the ginger, half the ras al hanout or garam masala, half the coriander, the egg and cayenne pepper and seasoning. Mix together and chill while you make the sauce.

3 To make the sauce, heat the oil in a pan, add the remaining onion and garlic and fry for about 5 minutes, or until softened. Sprinkle in the remaining turmeric and ras al hanout or garam masala and warm through.

VARIATION
Use a fresh lemon, instead of the preserved lemon, if you prefer. Cut it into small dice and add with the tomatoes.

4 Add the diced tomatoes, paprika and half the remaining coriander to the pan and cook over a medium heat until the tomatoes have formed a sauce consistency. Stir in the strips of preserved lemon.

5 With wet hands, roll walnut-size lumps of the fish mixture into balls and flatten slightly. Place in the sauce. Cook gently, for 15–20 minutes, turning twice. Garnish with coriander and serve with lemon wedges for squeezing.

VEGETARIAN AND VEGETABLE DISHES

The Jewish table has a tradition of vegetarianism.

When kosher meat is unavailable, or when there are no

kosher pans to cook it in, vegetarian dishes are often chosen.

In the cold Ashkenazi lands, vegetables would often be

shredded and baked into a kugel, although seasonal vegetables

such as squash and new potatoes could be cooked and served

with sour cream and herbs. The Sephardi kitchen was

abundant with vegetables such as (bell) peppers,

aubergine (eggplant) and pumpkin, which were often

stewed with olive oil, tomatoes and spices.

MEGADARRA

THIS DISH OF RICE AND LENTILS IS A CLASSIC MEAL FOR BOTH JEWS AND ARABS, FROM EGYPT AND LIBYA TO GALILEE AND GREECE. IT IS OFTEN ENJOYED WITH A BOWL OF VEGETABLES, ANOTHER OF COOLING YOGURT, AND A PLATE OF CRISP SALAD.

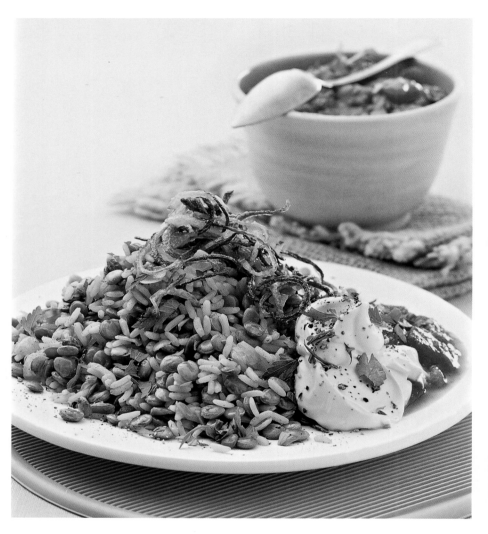

SERVES SIX TO EIGHT

INGREDIENTS
  400g/14oz/1¾ cups large brown or
    green lentils
  45ml/3 tbsp olive oil
  3–4 onions, 1 chopped and
    2–3 thinly sliced
  5ml/1 tsp ground cumin
  2.5ml/½ tsp ground cinnamon
  3–5 cardamom pods
  300g/11oz/1½ cups long grain
    rice, rinsed
  about 250ml/8fl oz/1 cup
    vegetable stock
  salt and ground black pepper
  natural (plain) yogurt, to serve

2 Heat half the oil in a pan, add the chopped onion and fry for 5 minutes, or until golden brown. Stir in half the cumin and half the cinnamon.

3 Add the fried onion to the pan of lentils with the cardamom pods, rice and stock. Mix well, then bring to the boil. Reduce the heat, cover and simmer until the rice is tender and all the liquid has been absorbed. If the mixture appears a little too dry, add some extra water or stock. Season with salt and pepper to taste.

4 Meanwhile, heat the remaining oil in a pan, add the sliced onions and fry for about 10 minutes, until dark brown, caramelized and crisp. Sprinkle in the remaining cumin and cinnamon just before the end of cooking.

1 Put the lentils in a pan with enough water to cover generously. Bring to the boil, then simmer for about 30 minutes, or until tender. Skim off any scum that forms on top.

5 To serve, pile the rice and lentil mixture on to a serving dish, then top with the browned, caramelized onions. Serve the megadarra immediately, with natural yogurt.

SUMMER SQUASH AND BABY NEW POTATOES IN WARM DILL SOUR CREAM

THIS IS AN ISRAELI DISH OF FRESH VEGETABLES AND FRAGRANT DILL THAT ARE TOSSED IN A RICH, BUTTERY SOUR CREAM SAUCE.

SERVES FOUR

INGREDIENTS

400g/14oz mixed squash, such as
  yellow and green courgettes
  (zucchini), and pale green patty pan
400g/14oz tiny, baby new potatoes
pinch of sugar
40–75g/1½–3oz/3–5 tbsp butter
2 bunches spring onions (scallions),
  thinly sliced
1 large bunch fresh dill, finely chopped
300ml/½ pint/1¼ cups sour cream
  or Greek (US strained plain) yogurt
salt and ground black pepper

COOK'S TIP
Choose small specimens of squash with
bright skins that are free of blemishes
and bruises.

1 Cut the squash into pieces about
the same size as the potatoes. Put the
potatoes in a pan and add water to
cover, with the sugar and salt. Bring
to the boil, then simmer for about
10 minutes, until almost tender. Add the
squash and continue to cook until the
vegetables are just tender, then drain.

2 Melt the butter in a large pan; fry
the spring onions until just wilted, then
gently stir in the dill and vegetables.

3 Remove the pan from the heat and
stir in the sour cream or yogurt. Return
to the heat and heat gently until warm.
Season with salt and pepper and serve.

SPLIT PEA OR LENTIL FRITTERS

THESE SPICY FRITTERS CALLED PIAJU COME FROM THE INDIAN SUBCONTINENT. THEY ARE, NO DOUBT, COUSINS OF TA'AMIA AND FALAFEL. SERVE WITH A WEDGE OF LEMON AND A SPOONFUL OF HOT, FRAGRANT CHUTNEY SUCH AS MINT.

SERVES FOUR TO SIX

INGREDIENTS

    250g/9oz/generous 1 cup yellow split
      peas or red lentils, soaked overnight
    3–5 garlic cloves, chopped
    30ml/2 tbsp roughly chopped fresh
      root ginger
    120ml/4fl oz/½ cup chopped fresh
      coriander (cilantro) leaves
    2.5–5ml/½–1 tsp ground cumin
    1.5–2.5ml/¼–½ tsp ground turmeric
    large pinch of cayenne pepper or
      ½–1 fresh green chilli, chopped
    120ml/4fl oz/½ cup gram (besan) flour
    5ml/1 tsp baking powder
    30ml/2 tbsp couscous
    2 large or 3 small onions, chopped
    vegetable oil, for frying
    salt and ground black pepper
    lemon wedges, to serve

1 Drain the split peas or lentils, reserving a little of the soaking water. Put the chopped garlic and ginger in a food processor or blender and process until finely minced (ground). Add the drained peas or lentils, 15–30ml/ 1–2 tbsp of the reserved soaking water and the chopped coriander, and process to form a purée.

2 Add the cumin, turmeric, cayenne or chilli, 2.5ml/½ tsp salt, 2.5ml/½ tsp pepper, the gram flour, baking powder and couscous to the mixture and combine. The mixture should form a thick batter. If it seems too thick, add a spoonful of soaking water and if it is too watery, add a little more flour or couscous. Mix in the onions.

3 Heat the oil in a wide, deep frying pan, to a depth of about 5cm/2in, until it is hot enough to brown a cube of bread in 30 seconds. Using two spoons, form the mixture into two-bitesize balls and slip each one gently into the hot oil. Cook until golden brown on the underside, then turn and cook the second side until golden brown.

4 Remove the fritters from the hot oil with a slotted spoon and drain well on kitchen paper. Transfer the fritters to a baking sheet and keep warm in the oven until all the mixture is cooked. Serve hot or at room temperature with lemon wedges.

DEEP-FRIED ARTICHOKES

CARCIOFI ALLA GIUDIA ARE A GREAT SPECIALITY OF THE JEWS OF ROME, NAMED AFTER THE ROMAN GHETTO GIUDIA. THE ARTICHOKES ARE PRESSED TO OPEN THEM, THEN PLUNGED INTO HOT OIL WHERE THEIR LEAVES TWIST AND BROWN, TURNING THE ARTICHOKES INTO CRISPY FLOWERS.

SERVES FOUR

INGREDIENTS
 2–3 lemons, halved
 4–8 small globe artichokes
 olive or vegetable oil, for deep-frying
 salt

1 Fill a large bowl with cold water and stir in the juice of one or two of the lemons. Trim and discard the stems of the artichokes, then trim off their tough end and remove all the tough outer leaves until you reach the pale pointed centre.

2 Carefully open the leaves of one of the artichokes by pressing it against the table or poking them open. Trim the tops if they are sharp. (Take care not to knock off the remaining leaves.)

3 If there is any choke inside the artichoke, remove it with a melon baller or small pointed spoon. Put the artichoke in the acidulated water and prepare the remaining artichokes in the same way.

4 Put the artichokes in a large pan and pour over water to cover. Bring to the boil and cook over a medium-high heat for 15 minutes, or until the artichokes are partly cooked. If the artichokes are small, cook them for only 10 minutes.

5 Remove the artichokes from the pan, place upside down on a baking sheet and leave to cool. When they are cool enough to handle, press them open gently but firmly, being careful not to break them apart.

6 Fill a wok or pan with oil to a depth of 5–7.5cm/2–3in and heat until hot.

7 Add one or two artichokes to the oil, with the leaves uppermost, and press down with a slotted spoon to open up the leaves, being careful not to splash the hot oil. Fry for 5–8 minutes, turning, until golden and crisp. Remove from the pan, and drain on kitchen paper. Serve immediately or place on a baking sheet and keep warm in the oven.

COOK'S TIPS
If you like, prepare and boil the artichokes ahead and deep-fry just before serving.

Stuffed Vine Leaves with Cumin, Lemon and Herbs

The important ingredients in these stuffed vine leaves are the flavourings and fresh herbs that give the brown rice filling its zest and special taste.

SERVES SIX TO EIGHT

INGREDIENTS
  250g/9oz/1¼ cups brown rice
  30–45ml/2–3 tbsp natural
    (plain) yogurt
  3 garlic cloves, chopped
  1 egg, lightly beaten
  5–10ml/1–2 tsp ground cumin
  2.5ml/½ tsp ground cinnamon
  several handfuls of raisins
  3–4 spring onions (scallions),
    thinly sliced
  ½ bunch fresh mint or 10ml/2 tsp
    dried mint, plus extra to garnish
  about 25 preserved or fresh
    vine leaves
  salt, if necessary
For cooking
  8–10 unpeeled garlic cloves
  juice of ½–1 lemon
  90ml/6 tbsp olive oil
For serving
  1 lemon, cut into wedges or half slices
  15–25 Greek black olives
  150ml/¼ pint/⅔ cup natural
    (plain) yogurt

1 Put the rice in a pan with 300ml/ ½ pint/1¼ cups water. Bring to the boil, reduce the heat, cover and simmer for 30 minutes, or until just tender. Drain well and leave to cool slightly.

2 Put the cooked rice in a bowl, add the yogurt, garlic, egg, ground cumin and cinnamon, raisins, spring onions and mint and mix together.

3 If you are using preserved vine leaves, rinse them well. If using fresh vine leaves, blanch in salted boiling water for 2–3 minutes, then rinse under cold water and drain.

VARIATIONS
For a twist to the classic stuffed vine leaf, other herbs such as dill or parsley can be used, and a handful of pine nuts can be added to the stuffing.

4 Lay the leaves on a board, shiny side down. Place 15–30ml/1–2 tbsp of the mixture near the stalk of each leaf. Fold each one up, starting at the bottom, then the sides, and finally rolling up towards the top to enclose the filling.

5 Carefully layer the rolls in a steamer and stud with the whole garlic cloves. Fill the base of the steamer with water and drizzle the lemon juice and olive oil evenly over the rolls.

6 Cover the steamer tightly and cook over a medium-high heat for about 40 minutes, adding more water to the steamer if necessary.

7 Remove the steamer from the heat and set aside to cool slightly. Arrange the vine leaves on a serving dish and serve hot or, alternatively, leave to cool further. Garnish and serve with lemon wedges or half slices, olives, and a bowl of yogurt, for dipping.

HATZILIM PILPEL

IN HEBREW, THE WORD HATZILIM MEANS AUBERGINE AND PILPEL MEANS SPICY AND PEPPERY. IN THIS RECIPE THEY COMBINE TO MAKE A FIERY TOMATO AND AUBERGINE STEW THAT IS TYPICAL OF ISRAELI COOKING, FOR WHICH AUBERGINES AND ALL THINGS HOT AND SPICY ARE STAPLES.

SERVES FOUR TO SIX

INGREDIENTS
about 60ml/4 tbsp olive oil
1 large aubergine (eggplant) cut
    into bitesize chunks
2 onions, thinly sliced
3–5 garlic cloves, chopped
1–2 green (bell) peppers, thinly
    sliced or chopped
1–2 fresh hot chillies, chopped
4 fresh or canned tomatoes, diced
30–45ml/2–3 tbsp tomato purée
    (paste), if using fresh tomatoes
5ml/1 tsp ground turmeric
pinch of curry powder or
    ras al hanout
cayenne pepper, to taste
400g/14oz can chickpeas, drained
    and rinsed
juice of ½–1 lemon
30–45ml/2–3 tbsp chopped fresh
    coriander (cilantro) leaves
salt

2 Heat the remaining oil in the pan, add the onions, garlic, peppers and chillies and fry until softened. Add the diced tomatoes, tomato purée, if using, spices and salt, and cook, stirring, until the mixture is of a sauce consistency. Add a little water if necessary.

3 Add the chickpeas to the sauce and cook for about 5 minutes, then add the aubergine, stir to mix and cook for 5–10 minutes until the flavours are well combined. Add lemon juice to taste, then add the coriander leaves. Chill before serving.

1 Heat half the oil in a frying pan, add the aubergine chunks and fry until brown, adding more oil if necessary. When cooked, transfer the aubergine to a strainer, standing over a bowl, and leave to drain.

VARIATION
To make a Middle Eastern-style ratatouille, cut 2 courgettes (zucchini) and one red (bell) pepper into chunks. Add to the pan with the onions and garlic and continue as before.

LEEK FRITTERS

THESE CRISPY FRIED MORSELS FEATURE PROMINENTLY IN THE SEPHARDI KITCHEN. LEGEND HAS IT THAT THESE WERE WHAT THE FLEEING ISRAELITES WERE MISSING AND MOANING FOR WHEN THEY WERE IN THE DESERT. THEY ARE BEST SERVED AT ROOM TEMPERATURE WITH A GOOD SQUEEZE OF LEMON JUICE AND A SPRINKLING OF SALT.

SERVES FOUR

INGREDIENTS

4 large leeks, total weight about
  1kg/2¼lb, thickly sliced
120–175ml/4–6fl oz/½–¾ cup
  coarse matzo meal
2 eggs, lightly beaten
large pinch of dried thyme
  or basil
freshly grated nutmeg
olive or vegetable oil, for
  shallow frying
salt and ground black pepper
lemon wedges, to serve

1 Cook the leeks in salted boiling water for 5 minutes, or until just tender and bright green. Drain and leave to cool.

2 Chop the leeks roughly. Put in a bowl and combine with the matzo meal, eggs, herbs, nutmeg and seasoning.

3 Heat 5mm/¼in oil in a frying pan. Using two tablespoons, carefully spoon the leek mixture into the hot oil. Cook over a medium-high heat until golden brown on the underside, then turn and cook the second side. Drain on kitchen paper. Cook the rest of the mixture, adding oil if needed. Serve with lemon wedges and salt.

VARIATIONS
To make spinach or chard fritters, replace the leeks with 400–500g/ 14oz–1¼lb fresh spinach or chard leaves and 1 finely chopped onion. Cook the spinach or chard leaves, in only the water that clings to their leaves after washing, until wilted. Leave to cool, reserving the cooking liquid. Roughly chop the greens and continue as in the recipe above, adding enough of the cooking liquid to make a thick batter.

SEPHARDI SPICY CABBAGE WITH TOMATOES, TURMERIC AND PEPPERS

THIS DISH OF HUMBLE CABBAGE IS FAR MORE EXCITING THAN YOU COULD IMAGINE AND NOT ONE TO PASS BY. THE LEAVES BECOME SILKY, FROM BEING THINLY SLICED AND PAR-BOILED, AND SPICY AND COMPLEX WHEN COOKED WITH YEMENITE-INSPIRED SPICING.

SERVES FOUR TO SIX

INGREDIENTS

1 green or white cabbage,
  thinly sliced
30–60ml/2–4 tbsp olive oil
2 onions, chopped
5–8 garlic cloves, chopped
½ green (bell) pepper, chopped
2.5ml/½ tsp curry powder
2.5ml/½ tsp ground cumin
2.5ml/½ tsp ground turmeric,
  or more to taste
seeds from 3–5 cardamom pods
1 mild fresh chilli, chopped, or
  2–3 pinches of dried chilli flakes
400g/14oz can tomatoes
pinch of sugar
juice of ½–1 lemon
45–60ml/3–4 tbsp chopped fresh
  coriander (cilantro) leaves

1 Cook the cabbage in a pan of boiling water for 5–8 minutes, or until tender. Drain well and set aside.

2 Meanwhile, heat the oil in a pan, add the onions and fry until softened, then add half the garlic and the green pepper and cook for 3–4 minutes, or until the pepper softens but the garlic does not turn brown.

VARIATION
Pan-fry meatballs until browned all over, then add them to the cabbage with the tomatoes and cook as above.

3 Sprinkle all the spices into the pan, stir and cook for 1–2 minutes to bring out their flavour. Add the reserved cabbage, the tomatoes and sugar, cover the pan and cook over a low heat for 15–30 minutes, or until the sauce is thick and flavoursome. If necessary, remove the lid and cook off any excess liquid.

4 Add the lemon juice and remaining garlic to the cabbage and cook for about 10 minutes. Stir in the chopped coriander and serve immediately. If you prefer, leave the cabbage to cool slightly before serving the dish warm. Alternatively, cool completely, then chill and serve as a cold salad.

TZIMMES

This is a baked dish of vegetables and dried fruit, although sometimes fresh apples and pears are added. Some tzimmes also contain meat and can be served as a main dish rather than as an accompaniment. The Yiddish expression gantze tzimmes, *meaning a "big deal", is inspired by this dish, which is full of rich, sweet and spicy flavours.*

SERVES SIX

INGREDIENTS
    250g/9oz carrots, peeled and sliced
    1 sweet potato, peeled and cut
        into chunks
    1 potato, peeled and cut into chunks
    pinch of sugar
    25g/1oz/2 tbsp butter or 30ml/2 tbsp
        rendered chicken fat or vegetable oil
    1 onion, chopped
    10 pitted prunes, halved
        or quartered
    30–45ml/2–3 tbsp currants
    5 dried apricots, roughly chopped, or
        30ml/2 tbsp sultanas (golden raisins)
    30ml/2 tbsp honey
    5–10ml/1–2 tsp chopped fresh
        root ginger
    1 cinnamon stick or 2–3 shakes of
        ground cinnamon
    juice of ½ lemon
    salt

1 Preheat the oven to 160°C/325°F/ Gas 3. Put the carrots, sweet potato and potato into a pan of sugared and salted boiling water and cook until they are almost tender. Drain, reserving the cooking liquid, and set aside.

VARIATION
To make a meat tzimmes, braise about 500g/1¼lb beef, cut into chunks, for 1–1½ hours until tender. In step 2 use oil, rather than butter, and add the meat to the pan with the vegetables.

2 Heat the butter or oil in a flameproof casserole, add the onion and fry until softened. Add the cooked vegetables and enough of the cooking liquid to cover the vegetables completely, then add the remaining ingredients.

3 Cover the casserole with a lid and cook in the oven for about 40 minutes. Towards the end of cooking time, check the amount of liquid in the casserole. If there is too much liquid, remove the lid for the last 10–15 minutes.

GALILEE SALAD OF WILD GREENS, RAW VEGETABLES AND OLIVES

WILD GREENS WERE GATHERED IN GALILEE BY NECESSITY DURING TIMES OF AUSTERITY; NOW THEY ARE EATEN FOR PLEASURE AND HEALTH. SERVE THIS SALAD WITH LABNEH OR YOGURT CHEESE.

SERVES FOUR

INGREDIENTS
1 large bunch wild rocket (arugula), about 115g/4oz
1 packet mixed salad leaves
¼ white cabbage, thinly sliced
1 cucumber, sliced
1 small red onion, chopped
2–3 garlic cloves, chopped
3–5 tomatoes, cut into wedges
1 green (bell) pepper, seeded and sliced
2–3 mint sprigs, sliced or torn
15–30ml/1–2 tbsp chopped fresh parsley and/or tarragon or dill
pinch of dried oregano or thyme
45ml/3 tbsp extra virgin olive oil
juice of ½ lemon
15ml/1 tbsp red wine vinegar
15–20 black olives
salt and ground black pepper

1 In a large salad bowl, put the rocket, mixed salad leaves, white cabbage, cucumber, onion and garlic. Toss gently with your fingers to combine the leaves and vegetables.

COOK'S TIP
Try to find mixed salad leaves that include varieties such as lamb's lettuce, purslane and mizuna.

2 Arrange the tomatoes, pepper, mint, fresh and dried herbs, salt and pepper on top of the greens and vegetables. Drizzle over the oil, lemon juice and vinegar, stud with the olives and serve.

VARIATION
Instead of making yogurt cheese, mash a little feta into natural (plain) yogurt and serve this instead.

CHOPPED EGG AND ONIONS

THIS ASHKENAZI DISH, ALTHOUGH THE ESSENCE OF MODERN WESTERN DELI FOOD, IS ACTUALLY ONE OF THE OLDEST DISHES IN JEWISH HISTORY. SOME SAY THAT IT GOES BACK TO EGYPTIAN TIMES. IT IS DELICIOUS PILED ON TO TOAST OR USED AS A SANDWICH OR BAGEL FILLING.

SERVES FOUR TO SIX

INGREDIENTS
8–10 eggs
6–8 spring onions (scallions) and/or
  1 yellow or white onion, very finely
  chopped, plus extra to garnish
60–90ml/4–6 tbsp mayonnaise or
  rendered chicken fat
mild French wholegrain mustard, to
  taste (optional if using mayonnaise)
15ml/1 tbsp chopped fresh parsley
salt and ground black pepper
rye toasts or crackers, to serve

COOK'S TIP
The amount of rendered chicken fat or
mayonnaise required will depend on how
much onion you use in this dish.

1 Put the eggs in a large pan and cover with cold water. Bring the water to the boil and when it boils, reduce the heat and simmer over a low heat for 10 minutes.

2 Hold the eggs under cold running water, then remove the shells, dry the eggs and chop roughly.

3 Place the chopped eggs in a large bowl, add the onions, season generously with salt and pepper and mix well. Add enough mayonnaise or chicken fat to bind the mixture together. Stir in the mustard, if using, and the chopped parsley, or sprinkle the parsley on top to garnish. Chill before serving with rye toasts or crackers.

ISRAELI WHITE CHEESE AND GREEN OLIVES

THE DAIRY SHELVES OF ISRAEL BOAST AN EVER-INCREASING ARRAY OF CHEESES, FROM KASHKAVAL TO GOAT'S CHEESES AND MILD WHITE CHEESES SPIKED WITH SEASONINGS, SUCH AS THIS ONE WITH PIQUANT GREEN OLIVES. SERVE IT WITH DRINKS AND LITTLE CRACKERS OR TOAST, OR AS A BRUNCH SPREAD WITH CHUNKS OF BREAD OR BAGELS.

SERVES FOUR

INGREDIENTS
175–200g/6–7oz soft white
  (farmer's) cheese
65g/2½oz feta cheese, preferably
  sheep's milk, lightly crumbled
20–30 pitted green olives, some
  chopped, the rest halved or quartered
2–3 large pinches of fresh thyme,
  plus extra to garnish
2–3 garlic cloves, finely
  chopped (optional)
crackers, toast or bagels, to serve

VARIATION
Add 115g/4oz chopped smoked salmon
and 2 thinly sliced spring onions
(scallions) to the cheese mixture.

1 Place the soft cheese in a mixing bowl and stir with the back of a spoon until soft and smooth.

2 Add the crumbled feta cheese to the blended soft cheese and stir until thoroughly combined.

3 Add the olives, thyme and chopped garlic to the cheese mixture and mix well to combine.

4 Spoon the mixture into a bowl, sprinkle with thyme and serve with crackers, toast, chunks of bread or bagels.

TURNIP SALAD IN SOUR CREAM

THIS ASHKENAZI SALAD MAKES A DELICIOUS ACCOMPANIMENT FOR A DAIRY MEAL OR PART OF A SELECTION OF SALADS. TRADITIONALLY, IF TURNIPS WERE NOT AVAILABLE, LARGE RADISHES WOULD BE USED INSTEAD.

SERVES FOUR

INGREDIENTS

2–4 young, tender turnips, peeled
¼–½ onion, finely chopped
2–3 drops white wine vinegar,
  or to taste
60–90ml/4–6 tbsp sour cream
salt and ground black pepper
chopped fresh parsley or paprika,
  to garnish

VARIATION
Crème fraîche can be used instead of the sour cream, if you like.

1 Thinly slice or coarsely grate the turnips. Alternatively, thinly slice half the turnips and grate the remaining half. Put in a bowl.

2 Add the onion, vinegar, salt and pepper, toss together then stir in the sour cream. Serve chilled, garnished with a sprinkling of parsley or paprika.

TABBOULEH

This is a wonderfully refreshing, tangy salad of soaked bulgur wheat and masses of fresh mint, parsley and spring onions. Feel free to increase the amount of herbs for a greener salad. It can be served as an appetizer or as an accompaniment to a main course.

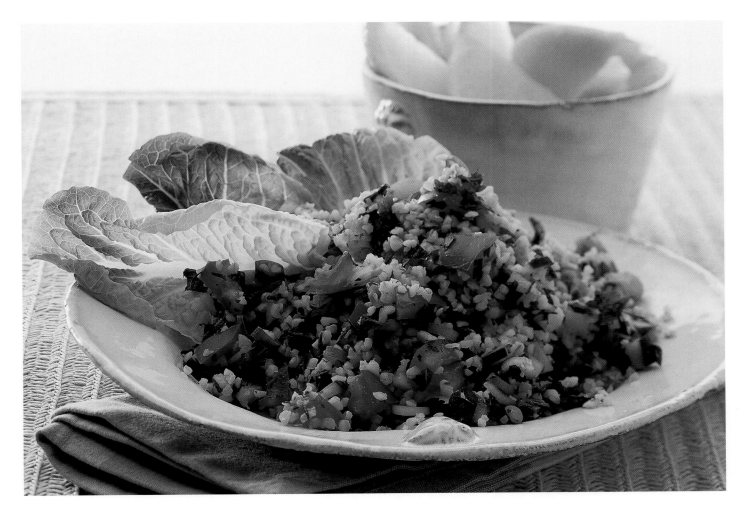

SERVES FOUR TO SIX

INGREDIENTS

250g/9oz/1½ cups bulgur wheat
1 large bunch spring onions
  (scallions), thinly sliced
1 cucumber, finely chopped or diced
3 tomatoes, chopped
1.5–2.5ml/¼–½ tsp ground cumin
1 large bunch fresh parsley, chopped
1 large bunch fresh mint, chopped
juice of 2 lemons, or to taste
60ml/4 tbsp extra virgin olive oil
salt
olives, lemon wedges, tomato wedges,
  cucumber slices and mint sprigs,
  to garnish (optional)
cos or romaine lettuce and natural
  (plain) yogurt, to serve (optional)

1 Pick over the bulgur wheat to remove any dirt. Place it in a bowl, cover with cold water and leave to soak for about 30 minutes. Tip the bulgur wheat into a sieve and drain well, shaking to remove any excess water, then return it to the bowl.

2 Add the spring onions to the bulgur wheat, then mix and squeeze together with your hands to combine.

3 Add the cucumber, tomatoes, cumin, parsley, mint, lemon juice, oil and salt to the bulgur wheat and toss to combine.

4 Heap the tabbouleh on to a bed of lettuce and garnish with olives, lemon wedges, tomato, cucumber and mint sprigs, if you like. Serve with a bowl of natural yogurt, if you like.

VARIATION
Use couscous soaked in boiling water in place of the bulgur wheat and use chopped fresh coriander (cilantro) instead of parsley.

POTATO KUGEL

THIS TRADITIONAL POTATO ACCOMPANIMENT CAN BE PREPARED WITH BUTTER BUT THIS RECIPE USES VEGETABLE OIL, WHICH GIVES A MUCH LIGHTER, HEALTHIER RESULT. THE USE OF OIL RATHER THAN BUTTER ALSO MEANS THAT THIS TASTY KUGEL IS PAREVE AND CAN BE ENJOYED WITH MEAT DISHES, FOR WHICH IT IS A PERFECT PARTNER.

SERVES SIX TO EIGHT

INGREDIENTS
  2kg/4½lb potatoes
  2 eggs, lightly beaten
  120–180ml/8–12 tbsp medium
    matzo meal
  10ml/2 tsp salt
  3–4 onions, grated
  120ml/4fl oz/½ cup vegetable oil
  ground black pepper

1 Preheat the oven to 200°C/400°F/ Gas 6. Peel the potatoes and grate finely.

2 Place the grated potatoes in a large bowl and add the beaten eggs, matzo meal, salt and ground black pepper. Mix together until well combined. Stir in the grated onions, then add 90ml/ 6 tbsp of the vegetable oil.

3 Pour the remaining 30ml/2 tbsp vegetable oil into a baking tin (pan) that is large enough to spread the potato mixture out to a thickness of no more than 4–5cm/1½–2in. Heat the tin in the oven for about 5 minutes until the oil is very hot.

4 Carefully remove the baking tin from the oven. Spoon the potato mixture into the tin, letting the hot oil bubble up around the sides and on to the top a little. (The sizzling oil helps to crisp the kugel as it cooks.)

5 Bake the kugel for 45–60 minutes, or until tender and golden brown and crisp on top. Serve immediately, cut into wedges.

COOK'S TIPS
• Don't be tempted to grate the onions in the food processor as the action of the knife creates a bitter flavour by breaking down the cells of the onions.
• For a dairy meal, this kugel can be made with any flavourful cheese such as Cheddar. Add about 350g/12oz/3 cups grated cheese to the grated potato and toss together, then continue as above.

THREE VEGETABLE KUGEL

GRATED SEASONAL VEGETABLES, BAKED UNTIL CRISP ON TOP AND CREAMY AND TENDER INSIDE, MAKE A WONDERFUL MODERN KUGEL. THIS VERSION COMBINES THE TRADITIONAL FLAVOURS AND METHOD BUT USES A MORE CONTEMPORARY COMBINATION OF VEGETABLES.

SERVES FOUR

INGREDIENTS

   2 courgettes (zucchini),
     coarsely grated
   2 carrots, coarsely grated
   2 potatoes, peeled and
     coarsely grated
   1 onion, grated
   3 eggs, lightly beaten
   3 garlic cloves, chopped
   pinch of sugar
   15ml/1 tbsp finely chopped
     fresh parsley
   2–3 pinches of dried basil
   30–45ml/2–3 tbsp matzo meal
   105ml/7 tbsp olive or vegetable oil
   salt and ground black pepper

1 Preheat the oven to 180°C/350°F/ Gas 4. Put the courgettes, carrots, potatoes, onion, eggs, garlic, sugar, parsley, basil, salt and pepper in a bowl and combine. Add the matzo meal and mix together to form a thick batter.

2 Pour half the oil into an ovenproof dish, spoon in the vegetable mixture, then pour over the remaining oil. Bake for 40–60 minutes, or until the vegetables are tender and the top is golden brown. Serve hot.

BREAD

Bread is one of the most important foods in the Jewish diet.
The variety of breads is staggering, from sweet and tender
challah eaten on Shabbat, to hefty sourdough ryes of Ukraine
and the flat breads of the Middle East. These breads are
usually made without milk or butter so that they may
be eaten with either meat or dairy meals.

PITTA BREAD

THROUGHOUT THE MEDITERRANEAN, PITTA IS THE MOST COMMONLY FOUND BREAD. THERE ARE MANY DIFFERENT TYPES FROM VERY FLAT ONES, TO THOSE WITH POCKETS, TO A THICKER CUSHIONY ONE. THE BEST PITTA BREAD IS ALWAYS SOFT, TENDER AND MOIST.

5 Heat a large, heavy frying pan over a medium-high heat. When smoking hot, gently lay one piece of flattened dough in the pan and cook for 15–20 seconds. Carefully turn it over and cook the second side for about 1 minute.

6 When large bubbles start to form on the bread, turn it over again. It should puff up. Using a clean dishtowel, gently press on the bread where the bubbles have formed. Cook for a total of 3 minutes, then remove the pitta from the pan. Repeat with the remaining dough until all the pittas have been cooked.

7 Wrap the pitta breads in a clean dishtowel, stacking them as each one is cooked. Serve the pittas hot while they are soft and moist.

MAKES TWELVE

INGREDIENTS
500g/1¼lb/4½ cups strong white bread flour, or half white and half wholemeal (whole-wheat)
7g packet easy-blend (rapid-rise) dried yeast
15ml/1 tbsp salt
15ml/1 tbsp olive oil
250ml/8fl oz/1 cup water

1 Combine the flour, yeast and salt. In a large bowl, mix together the oil and water, then stir in half of the flour mixture, stirring in the same direction, until the dough is stiff. Knead in the remaining flour.

2 Place the dough in a clean bowl, cover with a clean dishtowel and leave in a warm place for at least 30 minutes and up to 2 hours.

3 Knead the dough for 10 minutes, or until smooth. Lightly oil the bowl, place the dough in it, cover again and leave to rise in a warm place for about 1 hour, or until doubled in size.

4 Divide the dough into 12 equal-size pieces. With lightly floured hands, flatten each piece, then roll out into a round measuring about 20cm/8in and about 5mm–1cm/¼–½in thick. Keep the rolled breads covered with a clean dishtowel while you make the remaining pittas.

VARIATION
To cook the breads in the oven, preheat the oven to 220°C/425°F/Gas 7. Fill an unglazed or partially glazed dish with hot water and place in the bottom of the oven. Alternatively, arrange a handful of unglazed tiles in the bottom of the oven. Use either a non-stick baking sheet or a lightly oiled ordinary baking sheet and heat in the oven for a few minutes. Place two or three pieces of flattened dough on to the hot baking sheet and place in the hottest part of the oven. Bake for 2–3 minutes. They should puff up. Repeat with the remaining dough until all the pittas have been cooked.

PUMPERNICKEL

DARK BREAD WAS THE MAINSTAY OF MOST MEALS DURING THE CENTURIES OF JEWISH LIFE IN POLAND, RUSSIA AND THE BALTIC STATES AND MIGHT BE SPREAD WITH BUTTER, CHICKEN FAT OR SOUR CREAM, OR SIMPLY RUBBED WITH ONION OR GARLIC.

MAKES TWO LOAVES

INGREDIENTS

65g/2½oz plain (semi-sweet) chocolate or cocoa powder (unsweetened)
7g packet easy-blend (rapid-rise) dried yeast
200g/7oz/1¾ cups rye flour
300–400g/11–14oz/2¾–3½ cups strong white bread flour
5ml/1 tsp salt
2.5ml/½ tsp sugar
15ml/1 tbsp instant coffee powder
15ml/1 tbsp caraway seeds (optional)
105ml/7 tbsp warm dark beer
15ml/1 tbsp vegetable oil
90ml/6 tbsp treacle (molasses)
corn meal, for sprinkling

3 Make a well in the flour mixture, then pour in the chocolate or cocoa, 175ml/ 6fl oz/¾ cup water, the beer, oil and treacle. Mix well to form a dough.

4 Turn the dough out on to a lightly floured surface and knead for about 10 minutes, or until smooth.

5 Place the dough in a lightly oiled bowl and turn the dough to coat in oil. Cover with a dishtowel and leave to rise for 1½ hours, or until doubled in size.

6 Oil a baking sheet and sprinkle with corn meal. Turn the dough on to a lightly floured surface and punch down. Knead for 3–4 minutes, then divide the dough and shape into two round or oval loaves. Place the loaves on the baking sheet, cover with a clean dishtowel and leave to rise in a warm place for 45 minutes, or until doubled in size.

7 Preheat the oven to 185°C/360°F/ Gas 4½. Bake the loaves for about 40 minutes, or until they sound hollow when tapped on the base. Leave to cool on a wire rack.

1 Place a bowl over a pan of water and heat the chocolate or cocoa with 50ml/ 2fl oz/¼ cup water. Stir to combine, then set aside.

2 Combine the yeast, flours, salt, sugar, coffee and caraway seeds, if using.

BAGELS

THESE RING-SHAPED ROLLS ARE ONE OF THE EASTERN EUROPEAN JEWS' BEST CONTRIBUTIONS TO THE GASTRONOMY OF THE WORLD. THE DOUGH IS FIRST BOILED TO GIVE IT A CHEWY TEXTURE AND THEN BAKED. THE BAGELS CAN BE TOPPED WITH ALMOST ANYTHING: SCRAMBLED EGGS, FLAVOURED CREAM CHEESE, LOX OR FRESH, CHOPPED VEGETABLES ARE JUST A FEW EXAMPLES.

MAKES TEN TO TWELVE

INGREDIENTS
  7g packet easy-blend (rapid-rise)
    dried yeast
  25ml/1½ tbsp salt
  500g/1¼lb/4½ cups strong
    white bread flour
  250ml/8fl oz/1 cup lukewarm
    water
  oil, for greasing
  30ml/2 tbsp sugar
  corn meal, for sprinkling
  1 egg yolk

1 In a bowl, combine the yeast, salt and flour. Pour the lukewarm water into a separate large bowl.

2 Gradually add half the flour to the lukewarm water, beating until it forms a smooth, soft batter.

3 Knead the remaining flour into the batter until the mixture forms a fairly firm, smooth dough.

4 On a lightly floured surface knead the dough by hand for 10–20 minutes or, if using a bread machine, 5–8 minutes, until shiny and smooth. If the dough is sticky, add a little more flour. (The dough should be much firmer than ordinary bread dough.)

5 Lightly oil a bowl. Place the dough in it and turn to coat it completely in oil. Cover with a clean dishtowel and leave in a warm place for about 40 minutes, or until doubled in size.

6 Turn the dough on to a lightly floured surface and punch down with your fists. Knead for 3–4 minutes, or until smooth and elastic.

7 Divide the dough into 10–12 balls. Poke your thumb through each one then, working with your fingers, open the hole to form a bagel measuring 6–7.5cm/2½–3in in diameter. Place on a floured board and leave to rise for 20 minutes, or until doubled in size.

8 Preheat the oven to 200°C/400°F/ Gas 6. Bring 3–4 litres/5–7 pints/ 2½–3½ quarts water to the boil in a large pan and add the sugar. Lower the heat to a gentle boil. Lightly oil a baking sheet and sprinkle with corn meal. Beat the egg yolk with 15ml/1 tbsp water.

9 Add the bagels, one at a time, to the boiling water, until you have a single layer of bagels, and cook for 8 minutes, turning occasionally so that they cook evenly. Remove from the pan with a slotted spoon, drain and place on the prepared baking sheet.

10 Brush each bagel with the egg mixture. Bake for 25–30 minutes until well browned. Cool on a wire rack.

VARIATIONS
Add dried onions, garlic granules or poppy seeds to the bagel dough or top the bagels with poppy seeds, sesame seeds, caraway seeds, dried onion or garlic granules before baking.

CORIANDER AND CHEESE YEASTED FLAT BREADS

THESE FLAT BREADS ARE SALTY FROM THE HALLOUMI CHEESE AND ARE BEST EATEN WITH A LITTLE UNSALTED BUTTER, MIXED WITH CHOPPED RAW GARLIC, OR WITH A BOWL OF YOGURT SPRINKLED WITH GARLIC, AND WITH SPRING ONIONS, COS OR ROMAINE LETTUCE AND CUCUMBER SLICES.

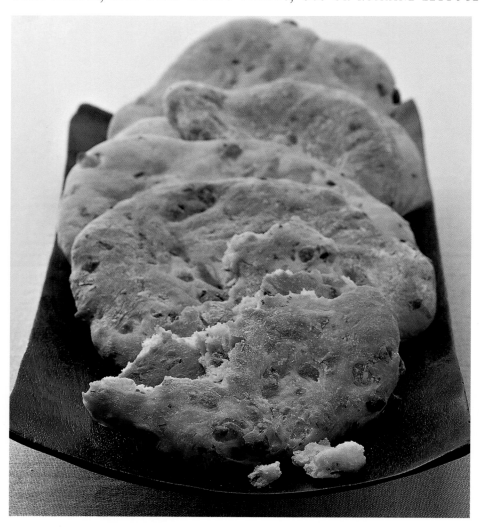

2 Knead the dough for 5–10 minutes until smooth. Lightly oil a bowl, place the dough in it, cover with a clean dishtowel and leave to rise in a warm place for about 1 hour, or until doubled in size.

3 Turn the dough on to a lightly floured surface and punch down with your fists. Knead in the cheese, then knead for a further 3–4 minutes.

4 Preheat the oven to 220°C/425°F/ Gas 7. Divide the dough into 10 pieces and shape each piece into a flat round about 1cm/½in thick. Place the dough rounds on non-stick baking sheets and leave to rise for about 10 minutes, or until doubled in size.

5 Bake the flat breads for about 15 minutes until they are risen and golden brown. Eat immediately.

MAKES TEN

INGREDIENTS
  500g/1¼lb/4½ cups strong white
    bread flour
  2 × 7g packets easy-blend
    (rapid-rise) dried yeast
  5ml/1 tsp sugar
  1 bunch fresh chives, chopped
  60–90ml/4–6 tbsp chopped fresh
    coriander (cilantro)
  45–75ml/3–5 tbsp dried onion flakes
  200ml/7fl oz/scant 1 cup water
  60ml/4 tbsp natural (plain) yogurt
  45ml/3 tbsp olive oil
  250g/9oz halloumi cheese, finely diced

1 Mix the flour, yeast, sugar, chives, coriander and onion flakes in a bowl, mixer or food processor. Add the water, yogurt and oil and mix to form a dough.

VARIATION
For a less salty result, use finely diced Cheddar in place of the halloumi.

ONION ROLLS

These sweet-smelling, tender rolls are based on those found in the Ukrainian bakeries of McAllister Street in San Francisco, which used to be like a tiny shtetl. Serve them hot, spread with butter, or cold, filled with sandwich ingredients, or eat with a bowl of warming soup for a satisfying lunch.

MAKES TWELVE TO FOURTEEN

INGREDIENTS
15ml/1 tbsp dried active yeast
15ml/1 tbsp sugar
250ml/8fl oz/1 cup lukewarm
   water
30ml/2 tbsp vegetable oil
2 eggs, lightly beaten
500g/1¼lb/4½ cups strong
   white bread flour
3–4 onions, very, very
   finely chopped
60ml/4 tbsp poppy seeds
salt

1 In a mixer fitted with a dough hook, a food processor fitted with a dough blade, or a large bowl, mix together the yeast, sugar and water. Sprinkle the mixture with a little flour, cover and leave for 10–12 minutes until bubbles appear on the surface.

2 Beat 5ml/1 tsp salt, the oil and one of the eggs into the mixture until well mixed, then gradually add the flour and knead for 5–10 minutes until the dough leaves the sides of the bowl. If the dough is still slightly sticky, add a little more flour.

3 Lightly oil a bowl. Place the dough in it and turn to coat. Cover with a dishtowel. Leave to rise in a warm place for about 1½ hours, or until doubled in size.

4 Turn the dough on to a lightly floured surface, punch down with your fists, knead the dough for 3–4 minutes, then knead half the onions into the dough. Form the dough into egg-size balls, then press each ball into a round 1cm/½in thick. Place on a baking sheet.

5 Lightly beat the remaining egg with 30ml/2 tbsp water and a pinch of salt. Press an indentation on top of each round of dough and brush with the egg mixture. Sprinkle the remaining onions and the poppy seeds on to the rolls and leave to rise in a warm place for 45 minutes, or until doubled in size.

6 Preheat the oven to 190°C/375°F/ Gas 5. Bake the rolls for 20 minutes, or until pale golden brown. Serve hot from the oven or leave to cool.

NEW YORK SEEDED CORN RYE SOURDOUGH

FORTUNATELY YOU DO NOT HAVE TO BE JEWISH TO LOVE THIS EASTERN EUROPEAN JEWISH BREAD. IT IS SURPRISINGLY EASY TO MAKE, ALTHOUGH YOU NEED TO PREPARE THE BREAD WELL IN ADVANCE AS THE STARTER TAKES A FEW DAYS TO FERMENT.

MAKES TWO LOAVES

INGREDIENTS
    1.6kg/3½lb/14 cups unbleached
        strong white bread flour
    7g packet easy-blend (rapid-rise)
        dried yeast
    250ml/8fl oz/1 cup lukewarm water
    60ml/4 tbsp caraway or dill seeds
    15ml/1 tbsp salt
    corn meal, for sprinkling
For the sourdough starter
    250g/9oz/2¼ cups unbleached strong
        white bread flour or a mixture of
        ¾ strong white bread flour and
        ¼ wholemeal (whole-wheat) flour
    7g easy-blend (rapid-rise) dried yeast
    250ml/8fl oz/1 cup lukewarm water
For the sponge
    200g/7oz/1¾ cups rye flour
    250ml/8fl oz/1 cup lukewarm water

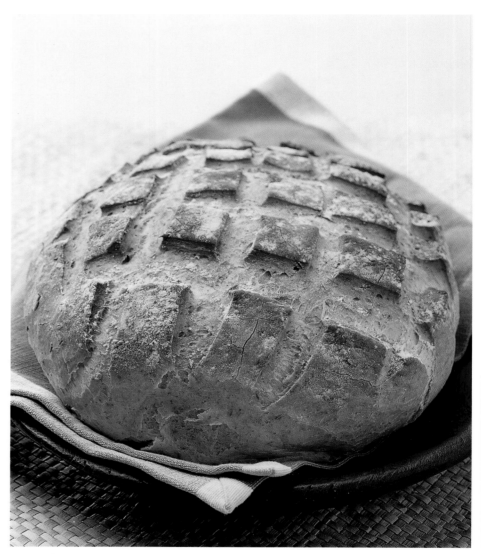

1 To make the sourdough starter, put the flour into a large bowl and stir in the yeast. Make a central well, stir in the water and mix together. Cover tightly. Leave at room temperature for 2 days or in the refrigerator for 1 week.

2 To make the sponge, put the rye flour into a large bowl, mix in the sourdough starter and water. Cover tightly. Leave at room temperature for 8 hours or in the refrigerator for up to 2 days.

3 Put the flour into a large bowl and add the sponge mixture, yeast, water, caraway or dill seeds and salt and mix to form a soft, slightly sticky dough.

4 Turn the dough into a large, clean bowl, sprinkle the top with flour, cover with a clean dishtowel and leave to rise in a warm place for about 2 hours, or until doubled in size.

5 Turn the dough on to a lightly floured surface and punch down with your fists. Knead for 3–4 minutes until smooth and elastic. Divide the dough in half, then shape each piece into a round loaf.

6 Sprinkle two baking sheets with corn meal. Place the loaves on the top and score each one with a sharp knife.

7 Cover each loaf loosely with a clean dishtowel and leave in a warm place to rise for about 45 minutes, or until doubled in size.

8 Preheat the oven to 220°C/425°F/ Gas 7. Fill a roasting pan with boiling water and place in the bottom of the oven. Alternatively, if you have a tile or pizza stone place this in the oven – it will help to create a thick, crunchy crust. Bake the loaves for about 35 minutes until lightly browned and hollow-sounding when tapped on the bottom. Cool on a wire rack.

CHALLAH

Sweet, shiny challah is the traditional braided Ashkenazi bread served at celebrations. Each Shabbat, it is challah that ushers in the observances, along with wine and candles. It is said that the shape resembles the hair of a Polish maiden for whom a baker had an unrequited passion — it was the most beautiful shape that he could think of for his bread.

MAKES TWO LOAVES

INGREDIENTS
15ml/1 tbsp dried active yeast
15ml/1 tbsp sugar
250ml/8fl oz/1 cup lukewarm water
500g/1¼lb/4½ cups strong white
  bread flour, plus extra if needed
30ml/2 tbsp vegetable oil
2 eggs, lightly beaten, plus 1 extra
  for glazing
pinch of sugar
salt
poppy or sesame seeds,
  for sprinkling

1 In a mixer, food processor or large bowl, mix together the yeast, sugar and 120ml/4fl oz/½ cup water. Sprinkle the mixture with a little flour, cover and leave for about 10–12 minutes until bubbles appear on the surface.

2 Beat 5ml/1 tsp salt, the oil and eggs into the mixture until well mixed, then add the flour, slowly at first until completely absorbed, then more quickly. Knead for 5–10 minutes until the mixture forms a dough that leaves the sides of the bowl. If the dough is still sticky, add a little more flour and knead again.

3 Place the dough in a lightly oiled bowl. Cover with a clean dishtowel and leave in a warm place for 1½–2 hours, or until doubled in size.

4 Turn the dough on to a lightly floured surface and knead gently, then return to the bowl. Cover and place in the refrigerator overnight to rise.

5 Turn the dough on to a lightly floured surface, punch down and knead until shiny and pliable. Divide the dough into two equal pieces, then divide each piece into three. Roll each into a long sausage shape.

6 Pinch the ends of three pieces together, then braid into a loaf. Repeat with the remaining dough and place the loaves on a non-stick baking sheet. Cover with a dishtowel and leave to rise for 1 hour, or until doubled in size.

7 Preheat the oven to 190°C/375°F/ Gas 5. In a bowl, combine the remaining egg, the sugar and salt, and brush over the loaves, then sprinkle with the poppy or sesame seeds. Bake for 40 minutes, or until well browned. Leave to cool on a wire rack.

VARIATION
To make challah for Rosh Hashanah, knead 200g/7oz/scant 1 cup glacé (candied) fruit or sultanas (golden raisins) into the dough before braiding. Sprinkle with hundreds and thousands before baking.

DESSERTS

No special meal would be complete without an indulgent
dessert, and there are plenty to choose from in the Jewish
kitchen, from crisp strudels to classic cakes. As a testament
to Jewish resourcefulness in adversity, some of the most
delicious, such as buttered challah pudding, are made from
the leftovers that would otherwise be thrown away.

POMERANTZEN

THIS CANDIED CITRUS PEEL IS A SPECIALITY OF JEWS WHOSE ORIGINS LIE IN GERMANY. AT FESTIVALS PEOPLE OFTEN OFFER A BOX OF POMERANTZEN AS A GIFT, USUALLY DIPPED IN DARK CHOCOLATE. THEY ARE EASY TO MAKE, AND APPEAL TO THE FRUGAL AS THE PEEL WOULD USUALLY BE THROWN AWAY, RATHER THAN BEING TRANSFORMED INTO SUCH A TREAT.

2 When the peels are cool enough to handle, gently scrape off as much of the white pith as possible. Cut the peel lengthways into narrow strips.

3 Put the sugar, water and golden syrup in a pan and bring to the boil. When clear, add the peels; simmer for 1 hour until translucent, taking care that they do not burn.

4 Stand a rack over a baking sheet. Remove the peels from the pan and arrange them on the rack. Leave to dry for 2–3 hours, then put in a plastic container or jar, cover and store in the refrigerator until required.

SERVES FOUR TO SIX

INGREDIENTS
   3 grapefruit and 5–6 oranges or
   6–8 lemons, unwaxed
   300g/11oz/1¾ cups sugar
   300ml/½ pint/1¼ cups water
   30ml/2 tbsp golden (light corn) syrup
   caster (superfine) sugar (optional)

COOK'S TIP
If you find it too much trouble to remove the pith from the fruit, omit this step, as once the pith has been simmered its bitterness fades.

1 Score the fruit, to remove the peels neatly, then peel. Put the peels in a pan, fill with cold water and bring to the boil. Simmer for 20 minutes, then drain.

5 If serving as a sweetmeat, cover a large flat plate with caster sugar and toss the drained peels in the sugar. Leave to dry for 1 hour. Sprinkle with sugar again and place in a covered container or jar. Store in a cool, dry place for up to 2 weeks or in the refrigerator for up to 2 months.

BUTTERED CHALLAH PUDDING <u>WITH</u> PEARS, CHERRIES <u>AND</u> ALMONDS

LEFTOVER CHALLAH MAKES SUPER BREAD PUDDING, AS ANYONE WHO HAS EATEN IT WILL AGREE. IF YOU PLAN TO SERVE IT AFTER A MEAT MEAL, USE FRUIT JUICE, SUCH AS PEAR JUICE, IN PLACE OF THE MILK.

SERVES SIX TO EIGHT

INGREDIENTS
75–115g/3–4oz/6–8 tbsp butter or
   pareve margarine, softened, plus
   extra for greasing
750ml/1¼ pints/3 cups milk
4 eggs, lightly beaten
2.5ml/½ tsp vanilla essence (extract)
2.5ml/½ tsp almond essence (extract)
1.5ml/¼ tsp salt
500g/1¼ lb leftover, slightly
   dry challah, thickly sliced and
   lightly toasted
130g/4½ oz/1 cup dried cherries
3 firm, ripe pears
200–250g/7–9oz/1–1¼ cups
   demerara (raw) sugar
130g/4½ oz/generous 1 cup flaked
   (sliced) almonds
cream, to serve (optional)

1 Preheat the oven to 190°C/375°F/ Gas 5. Butter a 25cm/10in square or oval baking dish. Mix together the milk, eggs, vanilla, almond essence and salt.

2 Spread the challah toast with butter, reserving 40g/1½oz/3 tbsp, then cut the challah into bitesize chunks.

VARIATIONS
To make an apple version, replace the almond essence with more vanilla essence and add 15ml/1 tbsp ground cinnamon to the milk. Use raisins or sultanas (golden raisins) instead of dried cherries, broken walnuts in place of the almonds, and apples instead of pears.

3 Add the buttered challah and dried cherries to the milk mixture and fold in gently so that all of the bread is coated with the liquid.

4 Core and dice the pears but do not peel. Layer the bread, sugar, almonds and pears in the dish, ending with a layer of sugar. Dot with butter. Bake for 40–50 minutes, or until caramelized. Serve with cream, if you like.

STRUDEL

THIS CRISP PASTRY ROLL, FILLED WITH FRUIT AND JAM, IS A CLASSIC ASHKENAZI SWEET TREAT TO ACCOMPANY TEA. NO ONE CAN RESIST A SLICE OF STRUDEL SERVED WITH A GLASS OF LEMON TEA.

MAKES THREE

INGREDIENTS
    250g/9oz/generous 1 cup butter,
      softened
    250g/9oz/generous 1 cup sour cream
    30ml/2 tbsp sugar
    5ml/1 tsp vanilla essence (extract)
    large pinch of salt
    250g/9oz/2¼ cups plain
      (all-purpose) flour
    icing (confectioners') sugar, sifted,
      for dusting
For the filling
    2–3 cooking apples
    45–60ml/3–4 tbsp sultanas (golden
      raisins) or raisins
    45ml/3 tbsp light muscovado
      (brown) sugar
    115g/4oz/1 cup walnuts,
      roughly chopped
    5–10ml/1–2 tsp ground cinnamon
    60ml/4 tbsp apricot jam or conserve

1 To make the pastry, beat the butter until light and fluffy, then add the sour cream, sugar, vanilla essence and salt, and beat together.

2 Stir the flour into the mixture, then put in a plastic bag and chill overnight or longer.

COOK'S TIPS
• Filo pastry dries out quickly, so always keep wrapped or covered when not using.
• To follow a meat meal, substitute the butter and sour cream with 120ml/ 4fl oz/½ cup sweet white wine and 120ml/4fl oz/½ cup vegetable oil.

3 Preheat the oven to 180°C/350°F/ Gas 4. To make the filling, core and finely chop the apples but do not peel. Put the apples in a bowl, add the sultanas or raisins, sugar, walnuts, cinnamon and apricot jam or conserve and mix together until well combined.

4 Divide the pastry into three equal pieces. Place one piece on a sheet of lightly floured greaseproof (waxed) paper and roll out to a rectangle measuring about 45 × 30cm/18 × 12in.

5 Spread one-third of the filling over the pastry, leaving a 1–2cm/½–¾in border. Roll up the pastry to enclose the filling and place, seam-side down, on a non-stick baking sheet. Repeat with the remaining pastry and filling. Bake the strudels for 25–30 minutes until golden brown all over.

6 Remove the strudels from the oven and leave for 5 minutes to become slightly firm, then cut into slices. Allow to cool, then dust with icing sugar.

RUSSIAN POPPY SEED CAKE

THIS PLAIN AND SIMPLE CAKE IS STUDDED WITH TINY BLACK POPPY SEEDS THAT GIVE IT A NUTTY, DISTINCTIVE TASTE THAT IS UTTERLY DELICIOUS. TRADITIONALLY CALLED MOHN TORTE, IT IS THE STAPLE OF RUSSIAN BAKERIES, WHERE IT IS SERVED WITH HOT TEA.

SERVES ABOUT EIGHT

INGREDIENTS
130g/4½oz/generous 1 cup
  self-raising (self-rising) flour
5ml/1 tsp baking powder
2.5ml/½ tsp salt
2 eggs
225g/8oz/generous 1 cup caster
  (superfine) sugar
5–10ml/1–2 tsp vanilla
  essence (extract)
200g/7oz/scant 1½ cups poppy
  seeds, ground
15ml/1 tbsp grated lemon rind
120ml/4fl oz/½ cup milk
130g/4½oz/generous ½ cup
  unsalted (sweet) butter, melted
  and cooled
30ml/2 tbsp vegetable oil
icing (confectioners') sugar, sifted,
  for dusting

1 Preheat the oven to 180°C/350°F/
Gas 4. Grease and base-line a 23cm/9in
springform tin (pan). Sift together the
flour, baking powder and salt.

2 Using an electric whisk, beat
together the eggs, sugar and vanilla
essence for 4–5 minutes until pale and
fluffy. Stir in the poppy seeds and the
lemon rind.

VARIATION
To make a poppy seed tart, pour the cake
mixture into a par-cooked pastry crust,
then bake for 30 minutes, or until the
filling is firm and risen.

3 Gently fold the sifted ingredients
into the egg and poppy seed mixture,
working in three batches and alternating
with the milk, then fold in the melted
butter and vegetable oil.

4 Pour the mixture into the tin and
bake for 40 minutes, or until firm. Cool
in the tin for 15 minutes, then invert
the cake on to a wire rack. Serve cold,
dusted with icing sugar.

KUGEL YERUSHALAYIM

THIS TRADITIONAL KUGEL THAT BEARS JERUSALEM'S NAME IS SAID TO HAVE BEEN BROUGHT TO THE RELIGIOUS QUARTER OF MEA SHEARIM IN THE 18TH CENTURY BY THE GAON OF VILNA AND HIS FOLLOWERS. IT IS EQUALLY GOOD CUT INTO SQUARES AND SERVED COLD FOR BREAKFAST OR TEA OR, MADE SWEETER BY INCREASING THE SUGAR CONTENT, FOR A HEARTY, SATISFYING DESSERT.

SERVES FOUR

INGREDIENTS
    200g/7oz very thin noodles, such as
        spaghettini or fine egg noodles
    60ml/4 tbsp olive oil
    130g/4½oz/⅔ cup sugar or
        demerara (raw) sugar
    2 eggs, lightly beaten
    5ml/1 tsp ground black pepper
    2.5–5ml/½–1 tsp ground cinnamon
    1–2 handfuls of raisins
    salt

1 Preheat the oven to 180°C/350°F/ Gas 4. Cook the pasta in salted boiling water according to the directions on the packet, or until just tender, then drain.

VARIATION
Add about 250g/9oz grated pumpkin to the noodles when adding to the caramel.

2 Put the oil and half the sugar in a large, heavy pan and cook over a medium heat, stirring with a wooden spoon, until the oil and sugar combine and the mixture turns light brown.

3 Remove the pan from the heat (the mixture will continue to cook and turn brown), pour over the pasta and mix well to combine.

4 Add the remaining sugar, the eggs, pepper, ground cinnamon, raisins and 2–3 pinches of salt to the pasta and mix well.

5 Turn the mixture into an ovenproof dish, 33 × 25cm/13 × 10in; spread into an even layer. Bake for about 1 hour, or until set and the top is lightly browned. Serve hot or warm.

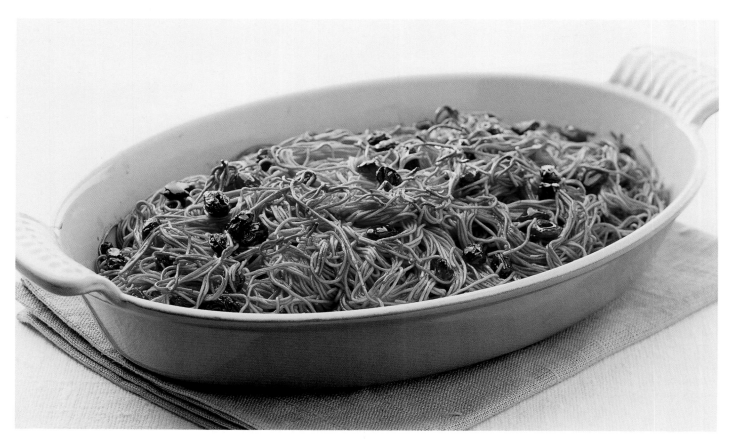

NEW YORK EGG CREAM

NO EGGS, NO CREAM, JUST THE BEST CHOCOLATE SODA YOU WILL EVER SIP. THIS LEGENDARY DRINK IS EVOCATIVE OF OLD NEW YORK. NO ONE KNOWS WHY IT IS CALLED EGG CREAM BUT SOME SAY IT WAS A WITTY WAY OF DESCRIBING RICHNESS AT A TIME WHEN NO ONE COULD AFFORD TO PUT BOTH EXPENSIVE EGGS AND CREAM TOGETHER IN A DRINK.

SERVES ONE

INGREDIENTS
   45–60ml/3–4 tbsp good quality
     chocolate syrup
   120ml/4fl oz/½ cup chilled milk
   175ml/6fl oz/¾ cup chilled
     carbonated water
   cocoa powder, to sprinkle

1 Carefully pour the chocolate syrup into the bottom of a tall glass.

2 Pour the chilled milk on to the chocolate syrup. Pour the carbonated water into the glass, sip up any foam that rises to the top of the glass and continue to add the remaining water. Dust with cocoa powder and serve. Stir well before drinking.

COOK'S TIP
An authentic egg cream is made with an old-fashioned seltzer dispenser that you press and *shpritz.*

PICKLES AND CONDIMENTS

Kosher dill pickles, resplendent with garlic and dill, are a
deli treat brought to America from Eastern Europe. But these
are not the only pickles in the Jewish kitchen. There is a wide
variety of relishes and condiments, including piquant chopped
salads and juicy preserved lemons. Hot peppers, herbs and
aromatic spices make up a grand array of condiments too,
from the fragrant halek of Persian Jews to the spiced chilli
sauces of Israel's Yemenite and North African Jews.

KOSHER DILL PICKLES

REDOLENT OF GARLIC, SALTY DILL PICKLES CAN BE SUPPLE AND SUCCULENT OR CRISP AND CRUNCHY.
EVERY PICKLE MAVEN (AFICIONADO) HAS HIS OR HER FAVOURITE TYPE.

MAKES ABOUT FOUR JARS

INGREDIENTS
  20 small, ridged or knobbly
    pickling cucumbers
  2 litres/4 pints/2 quarts water
  175g/6oz/generous ¾ cup kosher salt
    or coarse sea salt
  15–20 garlic cloves, unpeeled
  2 bunches fresh dill
  15ml/1 tbsp dill seeds
  30ml/2 tbsp mixed
    pickling spice
  ½ hot chilli, quartered

1 Scrub the cucumbers and rinse well in a bowl of cold water. Leave to dry.

2 Put the measured water and kosher or sea salt in a large pan and bring to the boil. Turn off the heat and leave to cool to room temperature.

3 Using the flat blade of a knife or a wooden mallet, lightly crush each garlic clove, breaking the papery skin.

4 Pack the cucumbers tightly into four 1.2 litre/2 pint wide-necked, sterilized jars, layering them with the garlic, fresh dill, dill seeds and mixed pickling spice. Add one piece of chilli to each jar. Pour over the cooled brine, making sure that the cucumbers are completely covered.

5 Cover the jars and leave to stand at room temperature for 4–7 days before serving. Store in the refrigerator.

COOK'S TIPS
• If you cannot find ridged or knobbly pickling cucumbers, use any kind of small cucumbers instead.
• If you have a dishwasher, prepare the jars by running them through on the highest heat setting.

PRESERVED LEMONS

THESE ARE WIDELY USED IN MIDDLE EASTERN COOKING. THE INTERESTING THING ABOUT PRESERVED LEMONS IS THAT YOU ACTUALLY ONLY EAT THE PEEL, WHICH CONTAINS THE ESSENTIAL FLAVOUR OF THE LEMON. TRADITIONALLY WHOLE LEMONS ARE PRESERVED BUT THIS RECIPE USES LEMON WEDGES THAT CAN BE PACKED EASILY INTO JARS.

MAKES ABOUT TWO JARS

INGREDIENTS
10 unwaxed lemons
about 200ml/7fl oz/scant 1 cup fresh
    lemon juice or a combination
    of fresh and preserved
boiling water
sea salt

1 Wash the lemons well and cut each into six to eight wedges. Press a generous amount of salt into the cut surfaces, pushing it into every crevice.

2 Pack the salted lemon wedges into two 1.2 litre/2 pint sterilized jars. To each jar, add 30–45ml/2–3 tbsp salt and 90ml/6 tbsp lemon juice, then top up with boiling water, to cover the lemons. (If using larger jars, use more lemon juice and less boiling water.)

3 Cover the jars and leave to stand for 2–4 weeks before serving.

4 To serve, rinse the preserved lemons well to remove some of the salty flavour, then pull off the flesh and discard. Cut the lemon peel into strips or leave in chunks and use as desired.

COOK'S TIP
The salty, well-flavoured juice that is used to preserve the lemons can be added to salads or hot sauces, such as zchug, horef and harissa.

TURKISH GREEN OLIVE AND TOMATO RELISH

THIS RELISH OF GREEN OLIVES IN A SAUCE OF TOMATOES AND SWEET PEPPERS IS WONDERFUL SERVED AT A BUFFET OR PICNIC WITH A SELECTION OF OTHER SALADS, OR ALONGSIDE A CRUSTY SANDWICH.

SERVES ABOUT TEN

INGREDIENTS
45ml/3 tbsp extra virgin olive oil
1 green (bell) pepper, chopped
  or sliced
1 red (bell) pepper, chopped
  or sliced
1 onion, chopped
2–3 mild, large red and green
  chillies, thinly sliced
1–2 hot, small chillies, chopped or
  thinly sliced (optional)
5–7 garlic cloves, roughly chopped or
  thinly sliced
5–7 tomatoes, quartered or diced
5ml/1 tsp curry powder or hawaij
1.5ml/¼ tsp ground cumin
1.5ml/¼ tsp turmeric
large pinch of ground ginger
15ml/1 tbsp tomato purée (paste)
juice of ¼ lemon, or to taste
200g/7oz/1¾ cups pitted or
  pimiento-stuffed green olives

1 Heat the extra virgin olive oil in a pan, add the chopped or sliced peppers, the onion and chillies, and fry for 5–10 minutes, or until the vegetables have softened.

COOK'S TIP
This relish is extremely popular in Israel and is particularly good with chunks of tuna fish as a cooling lunch on a hot afternoon. It is also good with cold pasta or a diced potato salad.

2 Add the garlic and tomatoes to the pan and fry for a further 2–3 minutes, until the tomatoes have become the consistency of a sauce, then add the curry powder or hawaij, the cumin, turmeric, ginger and tomato purée, then remove from the heat.

3 Stir the lemon juice into the mixture, then add the olives. Leave to cool, then chill in the refrigerator, preferably overnight, before serving.

CHOPPED VEGETABLE SALAD RELISH

THESE SALADS ARE BELOVED IN ISRAEL. THEY COMBINE THE FRESHNESS AND CRUNCHINESS OF THE SALADS ENJOYED BY THE ARABS WITH THE CHOPPED SALADS ADORED BY THE EASTERN EUROPEANS. IN SPAIN, TOO, CHOPPED SALADS ARE SERVED AS TAPAS, ESPECIALLY IN ANDALUCIA WHERE THE JEWISH AND MOORISH IMPRINTS ARE DISTINCT.

SERVES ABOUT FOUR

INGREDIENTS
2–3 ripe tomatoes, finely chopped
½ cucumber, finely chopped
½ green (bell) pepper,
  finely chopped
1–2 garlic cloves, chopped
2 spring onions (scallions), sliced
30ml/2 tbsp finely chopped
  fresh mint, dill or coriander
  (cilantro) leaves
30ml/2 tbsp finely chopped
  fresh parsley
grated rind and juice of 1 lemon
⅛ red cabbage, chopped (optional)
salt

1 Put the tomatoes, cucumber, pepper, garlic, spring onions, herbs and lemon rind and juice in a bowl. Mix together well, then chill in the refrigerator until ready to serve.

2 If using red cabbage, add to the relish just before serving, as its colour will run and spoil the fresh and vibrant colours of the other vegetables. Add a little salt to taste and stir to mix.

ZCHUG

THIS IS THE YEMENITE CHILLI SAUCE THAT HAS BECOME ISRAEL'S NATIONAL SEASONING. IT IS HOT WITH CHILLIES, PUNGENT WITH GARLIC, AND FRAGRANT WITH EXOTIC CARDAMOM. EAT IT WITH RICE, COUSCOUS, SOUP, CHICKEN OR OTHER MEATS. IT CAN BE STORED IN THE REFRIGERATOR FOR UP TO 2 WEEKS.

MAKES ABOUT 475ML/16FL OZ/2 CUPS

INGREDIENTS

5–8 garlic cloves, chopped
2–3 medium-hot chillies, such
  as jalapeño
5 fresh or canned tomatoes, diced
1 small bunch coriander (cilantro),
  roughly chopped
1 small bunch parsley, chopped
30ml/2 tbsp extra virgin olive oil
10ml/2 tsp ground cumin
2.5ml/½ tsp turmeric
2.5ml/½ tsp curry powder
seeds from 3–5 cardamom pods
juice of ½ lemon
pinch of sugar, if necessary
salt

1 Put all the ingredients except the sugar and salt in a food processor or blender. Process until well combined, then season with sugar and salt.

2 Pour the sauce into a serving bowl, cover and chill in the refrigerator until ready to serve.

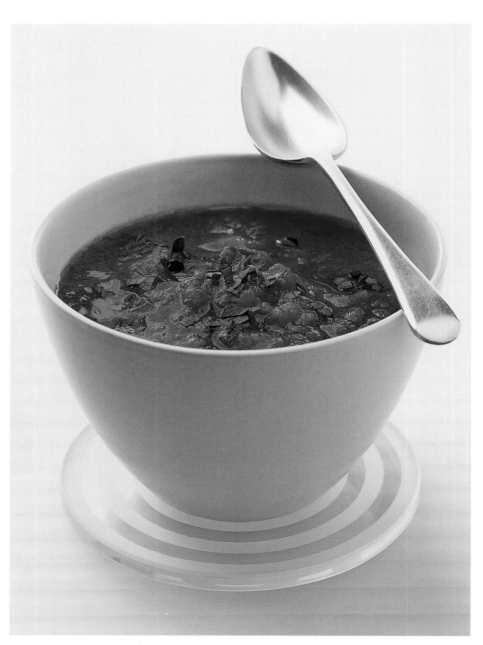

VARIATIONS
• To make a spicy yemenite dip, put 400g/14oz chopped fresh tomatoes, or a combination of chopped fresh and canned tomatoes in a bowl. Stir in 120ml/4fl oz/½ cup zchug, or to taste, and season with salt, if necessary. Spread the dip on to wedges of flat breads or serve in a bowl with strips of raw vegetables for dipping.

• To make hilbeh, a spicy tomato relish, soak 30ml/2 tbsp fenugreek seeds in cold water for at least 2 hours and preferably overnight. Drain, then grind the seeds in a spice grinder or pound them in a mortar with a pestle until they form a smooth paste. In a bowl, combine the paste with 15ml/1 tbsp zchug and 2 diced tomatoes. Season with salt and black pepper to taste.

FRAGRANT PERSIAN HALEK

THIS HALEK IS FRAGRANT WITH ROSE WATER AND THE SWEET FLAVOURS OF DRIED FRUITS AND NUTS,
WHICH ARE SO BELOVED BY PERSIAN JEWS.

SERVES ABOUT TEN

INGREDIENTS
60ml/4 tbsp blanched almonds
60ml/4 tbsp unsalted pistachio nuts
60ml/4 tbsp walnuts
15–30ml/1–2 tbsp skinned hazelnuts
30ml/2 tbsp unsalted shelled
  pumpkin seeds
90ml/6 tbsp raisins, chopped
90ml/6 tbsp pitted prunes, diced
90ml/6 tbsp dried apricots, diced
60ml/4 tbsp dried cherries
sugar or honey, to taste
juice of ½ lemon
30ml/2 tbsp rose water
seeds from 4–5 cardamon pods
pinch of ground cloves
pinch of freshly grated nutmeg
1.5ml/¼ tsp ground cinnamon
fruit juice of choice, if necessary

1 Roughly chop the almonds, pistachio nuts, walnuts, hazelnuts and pumpkin seeds and put in a bowl.

2 Add the chopped raisins, prunes, apricots and cherries to the nuts and seeds and toss to combine. Stir in sugar or honey to taste and mix well until thoroughly combined.

3 Add the lemon juice, rose water, cardamom seeds, cloves, nutmeg and cinnamon to the fruit and nut mixture and mix until thoroughly combined.

4 If the halek is too thick, add a little fruit juice to thin the mixture. Pour into a serving bowl, cover and chill in the refrigerator until ready to serve.

GLOSSARY OF TERMS AND FOODS

Adeni spice mixtures Adeni Jews have many different spice mixtures. The one for cooking is made of coriander, cumin, cardamom and pepper; the one for tea is made of cinnamon, cloves and cardamom; and the one for strong black coffee is made of ginger, cardamom, cloves and cinnamon.

Afikomen The piece of matzo, broken from the middle of the three matzos used at the Pesach Seder, that is wrapped and put aside to be searched for as part of the ceremony.

Ashkenazim Central and Eastern European Jews, including Yiddish-speaking Jews and their descendants.

Bagels Bread rolls with a hole in the middle, symbolizing the endless circle of life. They are boiled before being baked.

Baklava A crisp pastry of filo and nuts soaked in a honey syrup, which is often flavoured with rose or orange flower water or sweet spices.

Bar/Bat Mitzvah The coming of age ceremony for a boy (bar) or girl (bat) in which they assume the religious duties and responsibilities of an adult. A boy reaches this age at 13 years old, a girl at 12 years old.

Berbere The mixture of chillies and fragrant spices such as cardamom, black cardamom and ginger that forms the main flavouring of the Ethiopian cuisine. It is also the name of a certain type of chilli.

Besan See gram flour.

Betza/beitzah/baitzah Hebrew for egg. Betza are eaten by all Jewish communities and are considered pareve; they play an important role in the ritual plate for the Pesach Seder.

Betzel A Jewish North African cheese cracker, light and crisp, usually enjoyed for tea.

Bishak A Sephardi Bukharan pastry filled with pumpkin.

Blintz A thin pancake rolled around a savoury or sweet filling. They are often fried.

Borekas The flaky savoury pastries beloved by Turkish Jews. Borekas are usually half-moon shaped and have many different fillings. They may be made with filo dough, but a true boreka is made with a home-made dough.

Borscht Soup of Ashkenazi origins made from beetroot (beet) and sometimes other vegetables; it is eaten hot or cold.

Botarga Sephardi salted or smoked dried fish roe such as sea bass and grey mullet. It can be purchased or home-made; if purchased it should have certification to show that it is from a kosher fish.

Brik A deep-fried Moroccan-Tunisian pastry made from warka dough. Tuna and egg is a very popular filling.

Buricche Little Sephardi savoury pies of Italian/Turkish/Mediterranean origin. Fillings include chicken liver, tuna, pumpkin and chickpeas.

Challah The braided Ashkenazi Shabbat and holiday bread.

Chanukkah The festival of lights commemorating the Maccabean victory over the Seleucians in 165BCE (BC). Also known as Hanukkah.

Charosses/Charosset The paste of nuts, spices, wine and fruit eaten at Pesach to symbolize the mortar used by the Jews to build the pyramids. Also known as Harosset.

Chassidim A movement of very Observant Jews who originated in Poland, Ukraine and Galicia.

Chellou Persian rice, cooked with butter and allowed to form a crisp bottom crust. Vegetables, herbs, fruits and nuts may be added.

Chermoula A Moroccan spice and herb paste, often used with fish.

Chickpea flour See gram flour.

Cholent Ashkenazi, long-simmered stew of meat and beans. Adafina, dafina, hamim, cocido and skhena, are Sephardi equivalents.

Chrain Horseradish and beetroot condiment of Ashkenazi origin.

Chremslach Ashkenazi matzo meal pancakes, often eaten at Pesach. They may be savoury or eaten with sweet spices.

Dafina A long-baked Shabbat stew, made of beef (often with a cow's foot), potato, beans and hard-boiled eggs. It is a speciality of Moroccan Jews.

Dairy Refers to a meal made with milk products.

Desayuno Sephardi Shabbat breakfast.

Einbren flour Flour browned with fat. Traditionally, it is used to thicken soup in the German Ashkenazi kitchen.

Eingemachts A sweet preserve made from beetroot (beets), radishes, carrots, cherries, lemons or walnuts, eaten with a spoon along with tea. It is favoured at Pesach.

Etrog Large yellow citron used to celebrate Sukkot.

Falafel Deep-fried chickpea or broad (fava) bean croquettes, adopted from the Arabs. They are eaten with salads, tucked into pitta bread.

Farfel Pellet-shaped dumplings made from grated noodle dough or crumbled matzo.

Fassoulia White beans, often stewed with meats and vegetables, eaten as an appetizer or stew, popular with the Jews of Greece.

Fleyshig Yiddish for meals or products made of or prepared with meat.

Forspeizen Yiddish for a tasty appetizer.

Gefilte fish Ashkenazi balls of minced (ground) fish, eaten cold, poached and jellied or fried. *Gefilte* means stuffed, and originally the fish was stuffed back into its skin.

Glatt A particularly stringent form of Kashrut, favoured by Chassidic Jews.

Gram flour Also known as chickpea flour and besan. It is made from ground chickpeas and is used in Indian pakoras, spicy pastries, and falafel. It is also used in Mediterranean cooking: in Nice it is made into a pancake called socca and in Provence into cakes known as panisses.

Haimishe Yiddish for traditional home-made food.

Halek Date syrup, eaten for Pesach by the Jews of Iraq, India and Yemen, in addition to or in place of Charosses. In the Bible, "halek" is thought to refer to honey.

Halva A sweetmeat made from sesame paste and sugar or honey, and flavourings, then pressed into blocks and dried. Chocolate, pistachio nuts or almonds may also be added. Halva is popular with Jews from Middle Eastern and Balkan lands.

Hamantashen Triangular-shaped, Ashkenazi cookies with various fillings such as prunes, poppy seeds, apricots or nuts; eaten at Purim.

Hamim See Cholent.

Hanukkah See Chanukkah.

Harissa North African fiery paste of red chillies and spices, often served with mild foods such as couscous.

Harosset/Harosseth See Charosses/Charosset.

Havdalah The ceremony that marks the end of Shabbat and the start of the new week. Prayers are said over wine, special spices are smelled, and a braided candle is lit.

Hawaij A Yemeni spice mixture that includes cardamom, saffron and turmeric; used in most Yemenite cooking.

Helzel Yiddish for a stuffed chicken, turkey, goose or duck neck, filled with kishke stuffing and roasted so that the skin becomes crisp.

Hilbeh A pungent spice paste of soaked ground fenugreek seeds, often served with spicy zchug. Hilbeh is slighly bitter and has a unique aroma, almost like brown sugar. Yemenite in origin, it is eaten in Sephardi restaurants in Israel.

Holishkes Ashkenazi stuffed cabbage, often simmered or baked in a sweet-and-sour tomato sauce.

Horef Hebrew for hot pepper or spicy. Used in Israel to describe the spicy sauce or peppers eaten with falafel.

Huevos Haminados Sephardi long-cooked eggs; often placed in meat stews.

Injeera Ethiopian flat bread made from teff flour, a grain specific to Ethiopia. It is made from a fermented batter, which gives it a slightly sour flavour, formed into a huge pancake. It is used as a plate and pieces are used to pick up food.

Kaddaif Shredded dough used in Middle Eastern pastries to wrap around nuts, then baked and soaked in syrup.

Kaes The Yiddish word for cheese. Any dish that has kaes attached to its name has cheese as a component.

Kama A Moroccan spice mixture of pepper, turmeric, ginger, cumin and nutmeg, used for stews and soups.

Kapparot The symbolic ritual that takes place on the eve of Yom Kippur whereby a chicken is swung over the head and offered as ransom in atonement for a person's sins. Nowadays, a coin is often used instead of a chicken.

Karpas The parsley, lettuce or herbs placed on the Seder plate and dipped in salt water.

Kasha Toasted buckwheat.

Kashrut Jewish dietary laws dictating what may be eaten.

Katchapuri Flaky pastries filled with goat's cheese or feta cheese; brought to Israel from Georgian Russia.

Khoresht The sweet and sour Persian stew that is ladled over rice and features in the everyday diet of Persian Jews.

Kibbeh Dumplings of Middle Eastern origin made from minced (ground) lamb and soaked bulgur wheat eaten either raw, formed into patties and baked or fried, or layered with vegetables and baked.

Kichelach Light, crisp, slightly sweet cookies of Lithuanian Ashkenazi origin. They are traditional in areas where there is a large Ashkenazi population such as South Africa and the USA.

Kiddush Sanctifying blessing over the wine and challah.

Kindli Another name for Ashkenazi poppy-seed cake or mohn torte.

Kishke Stuffed intestine filled with matzo, chicken fat, onion and paprika. It is served roasted or poached.

Klops Meatloaf or meatballs of Ashkenazi German origin.

Knaidlach/Knaidl Matzo meal dumplings.

Knish Savoury pastry filled with meat, cheese, potato or kasha.

Kosher Term used to describe any food deemed fit to eat by the laws of Kashrut.

Kosher salt Large grains of salt for sprinkling on to meat, to drain out blood, as stipulated in the laws of Kashrut.

Kreplach Small meat-filled dumplings made of noodle dough, often served in chicken soup. At Shavuot they are filled with cheese and eaten with fruit and sour cream.

Krupnik Ashkenazi mushroom and barley soup. It is a traditional dish in Eastern European, particularly Poland, Lithuania and the Ukraine.

Kubaneh A Sephardi Shabbat breakfast dish cooked for a long time, often overnight.

Kubbeh Meat dumplings favoured by Iraqi Jews as well as those who emigrated to India and Israel. Kubbeh are eaten in soups and stews, and may also be steamed or fried.

Kuchen An Ashkenazi yeast raised cake that is slightly sweet and often stuffed with fruit. It is eaten with coffee or tea for morning or afternoon breaks, or as dessert for festivals or holiday meals.

Kugel Baked dish of noodles, vegetables, potatoes or bread; it may be sweet or savoury.

Lag b'Omer Holiday falling on the 33rd day of the counting of the Omer, the days between Pesach and Shavuot.

Lahuhua A Yemenite flat bread cooked in a frying pan. It has a crumpet-like texture and is eaten with soups and stews, often spread with zchug.

Latkes Fried potato pancakes eaten by Ashkenazi Jews at Chanukkah. Latkes can also be made with other vegetables or matzo meal.

Lekakh Traditional honey cake.

Lokshen Yiddish for noodles.

Lox Yiddish for smoked salmon.

Matzo meal

Lubia Black-eyed beans (peas), popular in Sephardi cooking, especially in Israel where they are added to spicy soups and stews.

Lulav The palm branch carried and waved as part of the Sukkot observance.

Mamaliga A creamy porridge-like mixture of corn meal, similar to polenta, eaten as the starchy staple by Romanians. It can be eaten hot or cold.

Mandelbrot Amond cookies resembling Italian biscotti. They are double-baked, giving a crisp, hard texture.

Mandlen The Yiddish word for almonds, which are favoured in Ashkenazi cooking (most famously in mandelbrot). Also the name of the crisp, baked or fried soup garnishes made from noodle dough.

Maror Bitter herbs eaten at Pesach/Passover.

Matjes herring See Salt herring.

Matzo/Matzah The unleavened, thin brittle bread ritually eaten during Pesach/Passover.

Matzo cake meal A fine flour made from crushed matzo, used to make cakes, cookies and other baked goods. Matzo cake meal may be used for Pesach, as long as it is labelled as matzo for Pesach.

A meal made from crushed matzo, used to coat fish and other foods for frying, bind together patties of meat, fish or vegetables and as the main ingredient for knaidlach. Matzo meal is available in medium or fine grade.

Megillah Scroll of the Book of Esther, read aloud at Purim as part of the observance.

Melawah Crisp North African pancakes made from pastry brushed with butter and rolled up thinly, similar to a Chinese spring roll pancake. When rolled out and baked, the layers puff up and become rich and flaky.

Menorah Also known as Chanukkia, the candelabra used at Chanukkah. It has spaces for eight candles, plus an extra in the middle, which is used for lighting the others.

Milshig Yiddish for milk or dairy, as opposed to meat.

Minhag Yiddish for different families' or communities' traditions and customs.

Mohn torte The Russian poppy-seed cake. *Mohn* means poppy seeds in Yiddish. See Kindli.

Mouna North African yeasted sweet tea bread, often stuffed with jam, served for Shabbat or a festival breakfast.

Muhammara A Middle Eastern paste of red (bell) pepper and bulgur wheat, particularly popular among Turks.

Nosh Yiddish, meaning to eat; can be a noun, meaning something to eat.

Oy Yiddish exclamation for any occasion: "Oy yoy yoy" and "oy vay s'mear" are variations.

Pareve Yiddish, describing the neutral foods that are neither dairy nor meat.

Pastrami A cured dried beef that is considered a speciality of the USA, though some say it was adapted from pastirma of Turkey, Romania and the Balkans. Traditional American pastrami is cured in salt, spices, pepper and garlic, then smoked and steamed.

Pesach/Passover The festival that celebrates the Israelites' exodus from Egypt.

Petcha Calf's foot jelly, a very traditional Ashkenazi dish that has now fallen out of fashion.

Pierogi Little pasta dumplings, of Polish origin, filled with fillings such as cabbage, mashed potatoes, onions, cheese and kasha and served with sour cream. The sweet, dessert version are varenikes.

Piroshki Ashkenazi savoury pastries of Russian origin made with a yeast dough and filled with cabbage, meat and hard-boiled egg, spinach and cheese, or kasha. They may be tiny, one-bite appetizers or large pastries, and either baked or fried.

Pitta bread Known as *khubz* in Arabic, pitta is a round flat bread that is cooked on a flat pan and puffs up as it cooks. The bread may be slashed open and its hollow inside filled like a sandwich. In addition to the pitta that we know in the West, there are many other pittas, for *pitta* simply means bread.

Plaetschen Ashkenazi term for little squares of pasta, which are eaten in soup.

Plava Very simple Ashkenazi sponge cake. It was once the favourite British Jewish cake and every bakery in London's East End had its own version.

Plotz Yiddish, meaning to faint, as in: "Oy, so delicious I could plotz!"

Pomerantzen Candied citrus peel, a classic sweet treat of the Ashkenazi Jews of Eastern Europe, especially Germany. Sometimes it may be dipped in chocolate.

Porge To ritually remove the blood and fat from meat.

Potato flour Used as a light and translucent thickening agent for sauces and cakes. It is popular during Pesach when grain flours are forbidden.

Preserved lemons A North African speciality, lemons are salted and layered in jars, which imparts a tangy flavour. They are often added to dishes such as tagines and salads.

Purim Festival celebrating the rescue of the Jewish people from Haman, as described in the Book of Esther.

Ras al hanout A Moroccan spice mixture that literally means head of the shop. Ras al hanout can contain myriad ingredients, and each spice shop guards its own secret recipe. For this reason, Kashrut is a consideration; many ras al hanout mixtures contain spices derived from insects or other ingredients that are not kosher. Check for a kashrut certification insignia.

Rosh Hashanah The Jewish New Year, literally meaning head of the year.

Rugelach Crisp, Ashkenazi cinnamon-and-sugar layered biscuits (cookies).

Rye bread A typical bread from Eastern Europe, especially Ukraine, where it is made with sourdough studded with caraway seeds. It is often baked on a corn meal-coated baking sheet and is, therefore, sometimes known as corn rye.

Salt herring Herring preserved in wooden barrels in layers of salt. Ashkenazi salt herring needs to be soaked in cold water before being eaten.

Sambousak Crisp half-moon pastries, of Sephardi Middle Eastern origin, often filled with cheese and hard-boiled egg, and coated in sesame seeds. They are popular in Israel and may be eaten hot or cold, dipped into zahtar.

Sauerkraut Fermented, pickled cabbage, made by salting shredded cabbage. It is a staple of the people of Eastern and parts of Western Europe.

Schav A refreshing, sour green soup made from sorrel and eaten cold. It is a traditional Ashkenazi soup and can be bought in bottles in American delis. It is sometimes referred to as green borscht.

Schmaltz Yiddish for fat, usually referring to rendered chicken fat.

Schmaltz herring See Salt herring.

Schnitzel Tender escalopes (scallops) of meat or poultry, coated in crumbs and fried. They originate from Vienna.

Seder The ceremonial dinner eaten on the eve of Pesach, commemorating the flight of the Jews from Egypt.

Sephardim Jews who settled in Iberia (Spain and Portugal), after the destruction of the Second Temple. This group, and their descendants, later spread to Greece, Turkey, the Middle East, England, the Netherlands and the Americas.

Shabbat The religious day of rest, which falls on a Saturday.

Shalach manot Food given at Purim. Shalach manot is often given to friends and family and people who are less well off.

Shalet Baked Ashkenazi dessert of apple and eggs, favoured by the Jews of Alsace. Other ingredients such as matzo, challah, dried fruit and spices may be added.

Shavuot Feast of the weeks, commemorating the revelation of the Ten Commandments.

Shochet The ritual butcher, licensed to slaughter and prepare meat according the laws of Kashrut.

Shtetl Yiddish for the Jewish villages of Eastern Europe.

Shulchan Arukh A code of Jewish law.

Simchat Torah The festival of the Torah, celebrated by parading the Torah through the synagogue.

Sour salt Citric acid, a souring agent used in Russia and in traditional Jewish cooking. It is available in crystals or grains.

Spaetzel Tiny dumplings made of noodle dough batter, dripped into boiling water. Also known as farfel, spaetzel.

Strudel Eastern European speciality of crisp, layered pastry filled with fruit, sprinkled with sugar and served as a mid-afternoon treat with tea. Strudel can be savoury, filled with vegetables, meat and sometimes fish.

Sufganiot Israeli jam-filled doughnuts, eaten to celebrate Chanukkah.

Sukkot The autumn harvest festival, the celebration of which includes eating meals in gaily decorated three walled huts known as sukkah.

Sumac/Sumak A sour-tasting, red spice made from ground berries of the sumac plant. Israelis, and some Sephardim, sprinkle the spice over salads, breads and rice.

Tahina/Tahini A Middle Eastern paste of toasted hulled sesame seeds, mixed with lemon juice, garlic and spices, and thinned with water. It is eaten as a sauce, dip, or ingredient in dishes such as hummus.

Tapadas Big Sephardi pies of Turkish origin, filled with a similar filling to that of Borekas. They are served cut into individual-sized pieces.

Teiglach Ashkenazi cookies that have been cooked in honey. They are a Lithuanian speciality, which are popular in communities that celebrate their Lithuanian origins, such as South Africa. They are favoured at Rosh Hashanah when sweet foods are eaten in hope of a sweet new year.

Tisha b'Av A mourning and fast day in commemoration of the destruction of the First and Second Temples in Jerusalem. It is observed on the 9th of the month of Av.

Torah The scroll used in the synagogue, consisting of the first five books of the Bible, which include the Ten Commandments. The Torah was given to the Jews by God on Mount Sinai.

Torshi Pickled vegetables, eaten throughout the Middle East, especially Persia. All kinds of vegetables are made into torshi, particularly turnips, which are pickled in a tangy vinegar and salt brine, with the addition of beetroot (beets) to give the pale-coloured turnips a bright pink hue.

Treyf Meaning not kosher. Also known as tref and trefah.

Tu b'Shevat Festival known as the birthday of the trees.

Tzimmes A sweet dish of carrots, vegetables, dried fruit and sweetening agent such as honey or sugar. Spices, and sometimes meat, are added.

Varenikes Ashkenazi fruit-filled pasta dumplings. They may be filled with apricots, cherries or prunes.

Varnishkes Noodles shaped like bow ties or butterflies, often served with Kasha.

Warka Very thin, transparent pastry from Morocco.

Wats/Wots Spicy Ethiopian stews, enjoyed by the Bene Israel (Ethiopian Jews). They are often eaten for Shabbat.

Yom Kippur The Day of Atonement, a solemn holy day upon which fasting is strictly observed.

Zahtar/Za'atar This is both the name of the wild thyme/hyssop that grows in the hillsides of Israel and the Middle East, and the name of the spice mixture made with it, which includes zahtar, ground cumin, toasted sesame seeds, coriander seeds and sometimes a little sumac and/or crushed toasted hazelnuts. Zahtar is eaten for breakfast, as a dip with fresh pitta bread, a drizzle of olive oil and fresh goat's cheese.

Zchug/Zhug/Zhoug This Yemenite seasoning paste is one of Israel's most popular spice mixtures. It may be red, based on chillies, garlic, spices, coriander (cilantro) and parsley, or it may be green, with more herbs and less or no tomatoes. Zchug is eaten as a dip with bread or as a relish or sauce.

Zeroa A lamb's bone, often a shank, roasted and placed on the ritual plate for Pesach. It represents the sacrificial lambs eaten on the eve of the flight of the Jews from Eygpt.

SHOPPING FOR JEWISH FOODS

Australia
Dainty Foods (Kravsz)
62 Glen Eira Road
Ripponlea
Melbourne VIC
Tel: (613) 9531 5032

Gefen Liquor Store
144 Chapel Street
Balaclava
Melbourne VIC
Tel: (613) 9531 5032

Grandma Moses Deli
511 Old South Head Road
Rose Bay
Sydney NSW
Tel: 371 0874

Kosher Imports
c/o Hebrew Congregation
13 Flemington Street
Glenside
Adelaide SA
Tel: (618) 9532 9994

Tempo Kosher Supermarket
391 Inkerman Street
St Kilda
Melbourne VIC
Tel: (613) 9527 5021

Canada
Avika's Kosher Food Market
3858 Bathurst Street
Toronto ON
Tel: (416) 635 0470

Bathurst Street Market
1570 Main Street
Winnipeg MB
Tel: (204) 338 4911

Capital United Kosher
  Market
5785 Victoria
Montreal PQ
Tel: (514) 735 1744

Glatt Kosher Self Service
215A St Louis
Montreal PQ
Tel: (514) 747 6531

Omnitsky Kosher
5866 Cambie Street
Vancouver BC
Tel: (604) 321 1818

South Africa
One Stop Superliner
217 Bronkhorst Street
Baileys Muckleneuck
Pretoria
Tel: (2712) 463 211

Saveways Supermarket
Fairmount Shopping Centre
cnr. Livingston
Johannesburg
Tel: (2711) 640 6592

United Kingdom
Amazing Grapes
94 Brent Street
London NW4
020 8202 2631

The Beigel Bakery
159 Brick Lane
London E1
Tel: 020 7729 0616

Brownstein's Deli
24A Woodford Avenue
Ilford IG2
Tel: 020 8550 3900

Cantor's of Hove
20 Richardson Road
Brighton BN3
Tel: 01273 596 500

Carmelli Bakeries
128 Golder's Green Road
London NW11
Tel: 020 8455 3063

J. A. Corney Limited
9 Hallswelle Parade
Finchley Road
London NW11
Tel: 020 8455 9588

Country Market Limited
136 Golder's Green Road
London NW11
Tel: 020 8455 3289

Cousin's Bakery
Golder's Green Road
London NW11
Tel: 020 8201 9694

Daniel's Bagel Bakery
13 Hallswelle Parade
Finchley Road
London NW11
Tel: 020 8455 5826

E & M Kosher Foods
24 Moresby Road
London E5
Tel: 020 8806 2726

A. Gee Deli
75 Pershore Road
Birmingham B5
Tel: 0121 440 2160

Greenfelds Kosher Foods
Greenfeld House
10–20 Windus Road
London N16
Tel: 020 8806 3978

Helen's Salt Beef Bar
43 Norwood Road
London SE27
Tel: 020 8670 8790

Kelmans Kosher Products
20 Stadium Business Centre
North End Road
Wembly HA9
Tel: 020 8795 0300

Kosher Paradise
10 Ashborne Parade
Finchley Road
London NW11
Tel: 020 8455 2454

L & D Foods Limited
17 Lyttleton Road
London N2
Tel: 020 8455 8397

Panzer Delicatessen Limited
15 Circus Road
London NW8
Tel: 020 7722 8162

J. Rogg
137 Cannon Street Road
London E1
Tel: 020 7488 3368

Sam Stoller and Son
28 Temple Fortune Parade
London NW11
Tel: 020 8458 1429

United Kosher Ltd
5 Croxdale Road
Boreham Wood WD6
Tel: 020 8953 5935

United States
The Challah Connection
19 Sunset Hill Drive
Monroe CT06468
Tel: (877) 426 8694

Empress Kosher
  Delicatessen
2210 86th Street
Brooklyn NY11214
Tel: (718) 265 8002

Kohn's Kosher Market
10405 Old Olive
  Street Road
St Louis MO63141
Tel: (341) 569 0727

Rubin's Kosher
  Delicatessen
500 Harvard Street
Brookline MA02446-2434
Tel: (617) 731 8787

World of Chantilly Inc.
4302 Farraght Road
Brooklyn NY11203
Tel: (718) 859 1110

BIBLIOGRAPHY

Avnon, Naf and Sella, Uri. *So Eat, My Darling; A Guide to the Yiddish Kitchen* (Massada Ltd, Israel, 1977)

Berenbaum, Rose Levy. *Rose's Melting Pot* (William Morros and Co, New York, 1993)

Bernadin, Tom. *The Ellis Island Immigrant Cookbook* (Tom Bernadin Pub, New York, 1994)

Cohen, Elizabeth Wolf. *New Jewish Cooking* (Apple Publishing, London, 1997)

Congregation B'nai Emuna. *The Kosher Gourmet* (self-published, San Francisco, undated)

De Silva, Cara (editor). *In Memory's Kitchen* (Jason Aronson, New Jersey and London, 1996)

Ehrlich, Elizabeth. *Miriam's Kitchen* (Penguin Books, New York, 1998)

Eley, John and Blue, Lionel. *Simply Divine* (British Broadcasting Corporation, London, 1986)

Fischer, Leah Loeb. *Mama Leah's Jewish Kitchen* (Macmillan, New York, 1990)

Fox, Rabbi Karen L and Miller, Phyllis Zimbler. *Seasons for Celebration* (Perigree Books, New York, 1992)

Friedland, Susan R. *The Passover Table* (Harper Perennial, 1994)

Friedman, Rose. *Jewish Vegetarian Cooking* (Thorsons Publishing, London, 1984)

Ganor, Avi and Ron Maiberg. *Taste of Israel* (Galahad Books, New York, 1993)

Ginor, Michael. *Foie Gras: a Passion* (John Wiley and Sons, New York, 1999)

Goldstein, Joyce. *Cucina Ebraica* (Chronicle Books, San Francisco, 1998)

Greenbaum, Florence Kreisler. *Jewish Cook Book* (Bloch Publishing, New York, 1926)

Greenberg, Florence. *Jewish Cookery* (Penguin Books, London, 1963)

Jackson, Judy. *Jewish: Traditional Recipes From a Rich Culinary Heritage* (Lorenz Books, London, 1998)

Jewish Fellowship of Davis. *99 Things You Always Wanted to Know About Jewish Cooking But Were Afraid to Ask* (self-published booklet, Davis, California, 1974)

Kasden, Sara. *Love and Knishes* (Fawcett Crest Books, Connecticut, 1969)

Krietzman, Sue. *Deli* (Harmony Books, New York, 1977)

Lebewohl, Sharon and Bulkin, Rena. *The 2nd Ave Deli Cookbook* (Villard, New York, 1999)

Leonard, Leah. *Jewish Cookery* (Crown Publishers, New York, 1949)

Levy, Faye. *Faye Levy's International Jewish Cookbook* (Ebury Press, London, 1992)

Machlin, Edda Servi. *The Classic Cuisine of the Italian Jews* (Dodd Mead and Co, New York, 1982)

Marks, Copeland. *The Great Book of Couscous* (Donald I Fine Books, New York, 1994)

Marks, Copeland. *Sephardic Cooking* (Donald I Fine Books, New York, 1994)

Marks, Gil. *The World of Jewish Cooking* (Simon and Schuster, New York, 1996)

Nathan, Joan. *The Jewish Holiday Kitchen* (Schocken Books, New York, 1988)

Roden, Claudia. *The Book of Jewish Food* (Viking Books, London, 1997)

Rose, Evelyn. *The Complete International Jewish Cookbook* (Pan Books, London and Sydney, 1976)

Rose, Evelyn. *The New Complete International Jewish Cookbook* (Robson Books, London, 1999)

Rose, Evelyn. *The Essential Jewish Festival Cookbook* (Robson Books, London, 2000)

Wolfert, Paula. *Couscous and Other Good Things from Morocco* (Harper Trade, 1987)

Author's Acknowledgements
Thanks to Alan "Kishke" McLaughlan, Dr Leah Spieler and Rev Jon Harford, Gretchen Spieler, Paula, Jojo and India Aspin, Dr Esther Novak and Rev John Chendo, Etty and Bruce Blackman, Jerome Freeman and the late Sheila Hannon, Paul Richardson, Nigel Patrick and Graham Ketteringham, Sue Kreitzman, Rabbi Mona Alfi, the late Rabbi Jason Gaber, so sadly missed, Katia Davies, Sandy Waks, Kamala Friedman, John and Mary Whiting, Fred and Mary Barclay, Amanda and Tim Hamilton Hemmeter, Gayle Merksamer, Antonietta Stefanic and her lovely girls Charlotte and Caroline, Faye Levy, Joan Nathan, Evelyn Rose, Josephine Bacon and Emi Kazuko who has now taken her first bite of Jewish food and fed me sushi in return; Susie Morgenstern and her sister Effie who took me to eat hummus in Jaffa and sent me to the best Romanian restaurants in Tel Aviv; my sister-in-law MaTao and my late brother Bryan Smith who preferred Chinese food to Jewish food, though he loved Kosher dill pickles.

My thanks to agent Borra Garson, associate Martine Carter and Michelle Waddsley who keeps the administration running smoothly; Miriam Morgen, Michael Bauer and Fran Irwin of the *San Francisco Chronicle* for letting me write about so many wonderful subjects, and *Saveur Magazine*, who sent me to Israel to write about falafel.

To my own Jewish family: parents Caroline and Izzy Smith (the famous baseball player, really!), aunt and uncle Sy and Estelle Opper, aunties Ella Smith and Sarah Rackusin who can rustle up latkes and cheesecake at the drop of a hat, and to my many cousins and nieces who are all good little eaters and good cooks too. As always, to Bachi for her love of good food, especially chicken soup, but this time she is sadly not here to enjoy it with me.

Publisher's Acknowledgements
All photographs are by William Lingwood except the following:
pp8, 10 bottom, AKG;
p9 The Bridgeman Art Library;
p17 David Harris, Jerusalem/ photo courtesy of the Beth Hatefutsoth Photo Archive;
pp10 top, 11, 13, 14, 16 top and bottom, Hulton Getty Images;
pp12, 15, The Jewish Museum, London.

INDEX